# Evolution of a Spirit

## One Man's Journey

### By Ken White

xulon
PRESS

Also by Ken White:

*World in Peril*

*We Wore Sterling Wings*

# Table of Contents

## Chapter 1 - From the Spirit

Faith in a Nutshell ................................................ 19
Adoration ............................................................. 20
The Garden .......................................................... 21
Mercy .................................................................. 22
Ending Vicious Cycles .......................................... 23
Belief ................................................................... 24
Love Poem ........................................................... 26
Death Be Not Proud .............................................. 27
He Died For Me .................................................... 28
Lies ...................................................................... 29
For Those Who Doubt ........................................... 30
Judgment ............................................................. 32
The Son of God .................................................... 33
The Holy Ghost .................................................... 34
Legacy of a Reformed Perfectionist ................. 35
Learning to Walk ................................................. 36
The Christian ....................................................... 38
Sharing ................................................................ 40
Universal Truth .................................................... 41
Romans 12:9 ........................................................ 42
Who Belongs to Him? .......................................... 43
Forgiveness .......................................................... 44
What Shall I Do? .................................................. 45
In His Presence .................................................... 46
Transformation ..................................................... 48
*Thundering Majesty* ............................................ 50

# Chapter 2 - Marriage & Divorce

In Truth ...............................................53
The Pearl .............................................54
The Last Goodbye ...............................56
Letting Go............................................58
Realization ..........................................59
Ruminations ........................................60
Love Poem II .......................................61
The Christmas Gift ..............................62
To Have and to Hold ............................63
Reconciliation ......................................64
Amends ...............................................65
Us........................................................66
Nick and Marguerite ............................67

# Chapter 3 - To My Child

Morning Breezes...................................70
Following..............................................71
The Unicorn .........................................72
The Flight of the Unicorn .....................74
A Night to Remember...........................76
Xana's Christmas ................................78
One Day While I Was Fishing ..............79
My Thunderbolt ....................................80
To My Child..........................................81
A Word to the Wise ..............................82
Verses..................................................83
Choosing a Mate .................................84

# Chapter 4 - War

Just the Facts......................................87
Identity Crisis ......................................88
Remembering Flanders Fields ............89
December 7th .......................................90
Bombing the Innocents .......................91
My First (B-52D) Bomb Run ...............92
Between Missions I .............................94

Between Missions II ........................................ 95
Remembering Vietnam ....................... 96
A Dying Breed ............................................ 100
The Final War ............................................ 102
The Real War .............................................. 108
La Croix ...................................................... 109
Epitaph ........................................................ 110

## Chapter 5 - Just for Fun

Dulcibella ...................................................... 113
Sam ................................................................ 115
Catnip .......................................................... 116
A Night at the Opera .................................. 117
Fizzgig Hits the Mark ................................ 118
Fizzgig's Reign of Terror ............................ 120
The Voters' Choice ...................................... 122

## Chapter 6 - Potpourri

The Choice .................................................. 126
Freedom of Speech ...................................... 127
Some Needs .................................................. 128
Freedom Isn't Free ...................................... 129
Behold, The Sparrow! .................................. 130
The Waging of Peace .................................... 131
When I Was Young ...................................... 132
Breaking the Curse ...................................... 133
PTSD ............................................................ 134
Sparky .......................................................... 136
Bart .............................................................. 138
Rocky (The Prodigal Cat) ............................ 140
The Gift ........................................................ 142
LITTLE GIRL .............................................. 144
A Fond Farewell .......................................... 145
At Little Vermillion ...................................... 146
Nicky ............................................................ 147
Deterrent ...................................................... 148
Freedom of Flight ........................................ 150
The Pass ........................................................ 151

Brotherhood ...................................... 152
Kitty Cats .......................................... 153
Renaissance Lady .............................. 154
Hopes For Heaven ............................ 156
On Eagles' Wings ............................. 158
Living Their Faith............................. 160
My Brethren...................................... 162

# Chapter 7 - Searching the Soul

Respect............................................. 165
Building Castles................................ 166
What I've Learned ............................ 167
Reconciliation II .............................. 168
Apologies.......................................... 170
Forgiveness: Ask and It's Yours....... 172
The Simple Solution ......................... 173
Ever Mindful.................................... 174
In God We Trust................................ 175
Time For A Change .......................... 176
The Solution to Loneliness ............... 177
The Presence .................................... 178
Just Desserts .................................... 179
Dare I Call You Father ..................... 180
The Lost Years ................................. 182
One Sleepless Night.......................... 184
Abuse ............................................... 186
As We Choose................................... 187

# Chapter 8 - Stories

The Wondrous Well .......................... 191
The Legend of E-ko-chee ................. 194
Rocky ............................................... 198
The Good Deed.................................. 202

Author's Note ................................... 203
Author's Biography .......................... 205

# Acknowledgements

First and foremost, I would like to give thanks to my beloved mother, Elizabeth A. White. Quite apart from my normal high school activities, she encouraged me to read the classics: Shakespeare, Shelley, Keats, etc. In doing so, she awakened in me a ravenous love of the English language, and for which I shall always be deeply indebted.

Among all of my high school English teachers, Mr. Patrick had a certain erudite flair in every aspect of the written creative arts. He instilled in me a strong desire to study and understand the writings of the celebrated English language storytellers, poets and essayists, and for which I am also indebted.

When I was at the Air Force Academy Preparatory School, Major John Galt spoke to us cadet-candidates in an unforgettable evening get-together. His love of poetry was infectious, and I soon dove headlong into writing poetry of my own.

I also wish to acknowledge my ex-wife, who shall remain nameless, to protect the innocent. She caused me to scour the depths of my soul; and, during our difficult period, gave me insights into writing poetry through which people in similar tragic circumstances may realize that they are not alone. She has remained a good sport throughout, and thus to her I owe a special debt of gratitude.

My brother, Richard, has, (and still does), challenge me to become greater than I would normally be, and reach higher than I normally would. I know it is his innate love and concern for me that prompts and motivates him, and for which I am truly grateful. As the Book of Proverbs says, "As iron sharpens iron, so one man sharpens another." (v. 27:17).

Many thanks go to my dear sister, Kathy, and her husband, Ed, a true officer and gentleman, for their unflagging support, many kindnesses, and occasional (much needed) brutal honesty, throughout all of my trials and tribulations.

If it weren't for my daughter, Stephanie, I might not have had any one to write many of my poems for, imparting what wisdom I could to her as a child of a broken home. I could only hope that I had made a difference, though she has turned out to be all that I could have hoped for in a daughter! Now, a generation later, these poems are also meant for my beloved granddaughters, Kyndra and Shelby.

I'm sure that my father, the late Maynard White, has had more influence on me that I could begin to realize. He has always set an example of dedication, integrity and determination; he instilled in me the importance of seeking excellence and of working hard in all one's endeavors. With his high regard for duty, he loyally served our country, often without the recognition he so deserved. To me, he will always be a great American.

My present wife, Marcia, a literal genius in her own right, has been infinitely helpful in encouraging me to continually utilize my abilities to benefit all. Her editing, proofreading and organizing skills have been indispensable. As much as my works are intended to discourage divorce, I'm convinced that Providence did indeed have a hand in bringing us together. I hope this work, as an object of so much of her support, may yet become as it was intended – a guide to living a Christian life in an uncertain and troubled world.

I have also received considerable editing help from my step-daughter, Rebecca; Marcia's sister, Andrea; and my pastor, Edgar Miranda; who helped in evaluating and choosing poems for the final draft. I also commend Gina Fleming of Xulon Press for her outstanding perseverance and patience in piecing together this book.

Perhaps, most of all, I would like to thank the myriad American servicemen, who have sacrificed in no small measure to keep our society free, so that high school kids can freely dabble in the arts.

Seeing their crosses row on row in Europe imparts a most profound feeling of dedication and self-sacrifice – agape, if you will, toward their fellow men for whom they were willing to lay down their lives. It was for these reasons, and the influence of my father, himself a dedicated career officer, that I became an Air Force pilot myself,— my most marvelous life experience, (this side of writing poetry).

# Introduction

The poetry and prose in this book have been in the works for over forty years; their roots were in Ken's childhood, combat experiences, and all the subsequent emotional ups and downs. The contradictory nature of his military career as a Strategic Air Command bomber pilot in Southeast Asia and later as a command post controller, with his more sensitive side, expressed through writing, music and acting, ultimately led to a PTSD-related breakdown and subsequent medical retirement. This was the end of what had been a promising military career. Not all wounds are physical, nor is all damage visible to the naked eye, but the hurt is just as deep, and the need for help not always easily recognized.

Ken's life spiraled downward; his marriage deteriorated, and eventually ended, giving him only limited time with his daughter. His interpersonal skills eroded, as did much of his common sense and judgment; leading him to be suspicious of loved ones, while trusting the untrustworthy. The prescription of contra-indicated medications exacerbated his physical and social problems; he became even more isolated.

From his initial psychotic break on, the bulwark between Ken and near-total withdrawal from the world was his faith in God and his growing relationship with Him. This is what opened him to seeking and accepting the medical and psychological help needed for his regenesis.

Many ups and downs populated Ken's continuing journey. False friends and deceitful business associates alternated with beloved family members, or fellow members of Emmaus, to temper him, and guide him down his path.

Ken has also discovered two new joys in his life, both totally unexpected. One is the everyday gifting to people in need, as they randomly cross his path ("That which you do to the least of thy brethren...").

The other is the joy of cats, playing with them, watching them, dancing attendance on them, and suffering the occasional (accidental) scratch, should he presume too much on their good nature. I myself have clearly seen that this "therapy" is as productive as any doctor.

This does not mean, however, that it is all clear sailing. There are still unreasonable attitudes, or occasional rages, triggered unexpectedly; there are times of self-pity, and moments of paranoia, but it gets better. It gets better for anyone who can accept that they need help, and seek it. Getting better, just like life itself, is an ongoing process; there is no _cure_ for PTSD, any more than there is for alcoholism, Bi-Polar Disorder, or diabetes. There is, however, treatment and hope; but it requires an ongoing commitment to working at the process of healing.

Ken's poem, "PTSD," says that he's "not quite right," and that's OK. He didn't ask for the emotional trauma that triggered his chemical imbalances, and he knows that it is not his fault. One of his primary reasons for publishing this book is to help spread this message to others: especially victims of PTSD, their friends and families, co-workers, and the world around them.

If you are uncertain about just where Ken's self-described "evolution" started, and the progress he has made so far, please read the following poem, one of his earliest, titled "Insanity?"

> I landed in a hospital,
>   Near rationally blind!
> I felt I had to tell someone
>   Of what was on my mind.

I cried in desperation
　　When I began to fear
That no matter what my story was,
　　No one cared to hear.

They seemed to have a policy,
　　Written neat and plain:
No one pays attention
　　When you're classified: Insane.

My message was important,
　　For all the world to know,
As it would help determine
　　The direction we would go!

If only they would listen
　　How Jesus Christ is Lord;
But they either showed amusement,
　　Or they seemed completely bored.

Life could be much better,
　　A fact I'm certain of,
If in the spirit and the letter,
　　We would show our neighbor love!

But with time and with their drugs,
　　It soon was plain to see
They wanted to return me
　　Back to their reality!

I now see two realities:
　　Mundane, and then, divine.
I sometimes wonder which is best,
　　Theirs, perhaps, or mine?

Ken White (2/25/81)

Remember, the first step of the journey is the hardest. Read the poems, follow Ken's journey as documented thus far; perhaps it will then be time to start one of your own.

Marcia White (2/20/12)

Author's introductory comments:

This book is about my spiritual awakening, conversion, and growth; followed by a belated discovery of love, compassion and concern for all of Humanity – a journey from death into Life.

Although this book details my journey, if others with similar experiences can benefit from it, I will feel blest indeed!

I might add that if, as we have been told, war is "merely an extension of foreign policy," then it would seem that there has to be a better way; and, I am certain that if we seek it earnestly enough, it shall be found (Matthew 7:7-8).

Ken White (7/31/12)

This book is dedicated
to Sparky, Elmo,
Lily, Dulcie,
Fizzgig,
Sam, and Rocky;
Who have given me
No end of joy.

# Chapter 1 - From the Spirit

I first asked for God's love and acceptance when I was an Air Force Academy cadet. While unaware of any response at the time, I felt certain that He understood.

The aftereffects of my two tours of duty in Southeast Asia cost me my life as I knew it. Like the Biblical Job, I lost everything: my marriage, my career, my daughter, my friends, the future I had envisioned, and, ultimately, my sanity. I had nowhere to turn, but to God; a relationship that thankfully grew and continues to grow.

During one of my several stays on psychiatric wards in various hospitals, I was infused with a driving desire to learn all that I possibly could about God and what He expected of me. I recall one nurse closing my Bible, setting it on the bedside table, and saying, "Let's put this away for now." When I showed any zeal toward God, the staff assumed that I had simply "lost touch with reality."

It was around then that I thought that memorization of Scripture was the answer; I had not yet learned the difference between "talking the talk," and "walking the walk." Ephesians 2:8-9 says, "You were saved by the Grace of God through faith, and that not of yourselves…that anyone should boast." It took me virtually thirty years to understand this, having spent most of that time vainly trying to *earn* Salvation and *work* my way into God's favor.

It was eventually revealed to me that Christ had done all of the work of our Salvation while on the Cross, requiring only our acknowledgment of Him as Savior to be saved! Thus I came to realize that I had belonged to God from the very moment I first called upon Him (Romans 10:13).

# Faith in a Nutshell

Original Poem by Ken White

Music Selected by Wayne Kastl

1. Some peo - ple miss the mes-sage that the Bi - ble un - der - scores:
2. O - pen up your heart to His; and let Him be your Lord;
3. He'll help you with your bur - dens; and lis - ten as you pray;

Yes, Je - sus is the Sa-vior, friend, but have you made Him yours?
Then seek to live with-in His will; there is a just re - ward!
And as you learn o - be - dience, He'll help you find the Way.

Then learn of His for-/give-/ness, and of His sa - ving Gra – ce,
And learn a-bout His stead-fast love, His gui - ding Spir - it, too,
Our faith is in His pro-mi-ses; Sal - va - tion is as - sur - ed!

For when He grants E - ter - nal Life, your sins He will e - race!
How when you give your life to Him, all things be - come a - new!
And that, though in a nut-shell, is the mea - ning of His Word.

# Faith in a Nutshell

Some people miss the message
     That the Bible underscores:
Yes, Jesus is the Savior, friend,
     But have you made Him yours?

Then learn of His forgiveness,
     And of His saving Grace;
For when He grants Eternal Life,
     Your sins He will erase!

Open up your heart to His;
     And let Him be your Lord,
Then seek to live within His will;
     There is a just reward!

And learn about His steadfast love,
     His guiding Spirit, too;
How when you give your life to Him,
     All things become anew!

He'll help you with your burdens,
     And listen as you pray;
And as you learn obedience,
     He'll help you find the Way!

Our faith is in His promises;
     Salvation is assured!
And that, though in a nutshell,
     Is the meaning of His Word!

(5/29/81)
Matthew 11:28-30

# Adoration

I come to You on bended knee,
  O Conqueror of Calvary!
For nothing more have I adored;
  O never leave me, Precious Lord!

What can I offer You that's mine,
  For all Creation's wholly thine?
I give what little I possess:
  My heart, my mind, my faithfulness!

For I have also tasted fear;
  I almost couldn't persevere!
Your strength and love will see me through,
  Until, at last, I am with You!

My Lord and Savior, God above,
  How can I thank You for Your love?
You cleansed me of my guilt and shame;
  Forever will I praise Your Name!

(11/18/81)

# The Garden

The greatest choice that ever was,
   And evermore shall be,
Was given to the Son of Man
   While in Gethsemane.

The choice He knew He had to make
   Weighed heavy on His mind:
Would He take upon Himself
   The sins of Humankind?

He didn't have to go along;
   The choice was His to make.
Would He take all sin to Hell,
   With all our souls at stake?

His prayer was ne'er so earnest,
   As sweat beaded on His brow;
"Abba, must I take this cup?
   All's possible with Thou!"

Then as the true, obedient Son,
   Whose Father He adores,
He uttered those momentous words:
   "Not My will, but Yours!"

This most wondrous of decisions
   Led to that curséd tree,
But the choice He made to die for us
   Gave Life to you and me!

(4/4/95) Matthew 26:36-42

# Mercy

I often have to remember my Lord,
    Oh, my wandering soul!
Yet with Him so often my heart has soared,
    And His Spirit has made me whole.

His pain and suffering brings me to tears
    When I think of what He had borne
On the cross that embodied our hopes and fears,
    Where He died amid mocking and scorn!

He took away all of our guilt and sin;
    Our souls He willed to save.
In believing in Him our lives begin,
    And continue beyond the grave!

The beauty is knowing that God is Love,
    And we can abide with Him!
Without that ascension to Heaven above,
    Our future would still be grim.

His Spirit is with our heart and mind,
    It will guide and direct and prod;
Until, when face-to-face, we will find
    We can say, "My Lord and my God."

(5/5/81)
1 John 2:28
John 20:24-29

# Ending Vicious Cycles

"Love your neighbor as yourself,"
        I know that path is best,
And yet I come up lacking
        When I put it to the test!

How am I to love someone,
        Yet hate the things they do?
Do you do unto another
        As they have done to you?

I know the cycle has to break;
        Forgiveness must prevail.
We must end up with love, not hate;
        In that we cannot fail!

I'll hope to show a loving heart,
        No matter how I feel;
Knowing God will help to make
        My aspirations real!

Jesus trod this narrow path.
        I'll follow where He led.
It's not enough to hear his words,
        But <u>do</u> what He has said!

(1/20/86) James 1:22-25

# Belief

There were those who on the battlefield
Once charged with lance or sword;
Prepared to risk their very lives,
But not to meet the Lord!

How many times before today
Have people come to grief,
Strong in constitution
But weak in their belief?

Many never knew of what
The Bible had to say,
And never saw its ray of Hope
Before their dying day!

Some are so preoccupied
With work or daily strife,
They never took the time to seek
Or find Eternal Life!*

Some knew religious doctrine
And tried to be devout,
But when they took the leap of Faith,
They stumbled on their doubt.

From worry, fear and doubt this Faith
Can offer us reprieve,
But before it can begin to heal –
First, we must believe!

Believe in all the Promises,
The Glory and the Power!
Believe the Lord will care for us
In each and every hour!

Accept the Wisdom of the Lord,
And put your mind to rest.
Faith will bring a great reward,
And you'll be ever blest!

He makes the path more obvious
Once you're on the way,
So, don't put off till tomorrow
What you ought to do today!

And as you let Him change your life,
Receive and feel His love;
You'll want to share it everywhere,
And praise the Lord above!

(1981)
John 6:28-29
*John 17:3

# Love Poem

If life is sad and lonely,
    And it seems so hard to live;
When love is what you want so much,
    And what you'd like to give;

Remember, God has loved you
    More than you'll ever know;
You have His love within your heart
    No matter where you go!

And when others are unhappy,
    And want to share your love,
Give what you have gotten
    From our Father up above!

For when you take God's love in you
    And give it all away,
You have more than you started with;
    It always works that way!

The world is what we make it,
    Whether dark or shiny bright;
And if it needs some brightness,
    Let it see your loving light!

(2/27/81)

## Death Be Not Proud

Jesus is Lord!
   Let us be not afraid!
For He 'rose from the dead
   In the tomb where he laid!

Both in life and in death,
   He has shown us the Way;
For what He has done,
   We can never repay!

Yes, Christ is our Savior!
   There's nothing to fear!
Now joy is the reason
   For shedding a tear!

We know we're forgiven
   For all of our sins,
When through faith in the Lord,
   Life Eternal begins!

For Heaven is something
   No man can achieve,
But is only attained
   When in Christ we believe!

We're raised from the dead, then,
   In more ways than one,
By casting our fate with
   God's only Son!

(1991)
John 3:16
John 8:51

# He Died For Me

You wonder how my life was changed,
   And why I'm hopeful now:
He died for me! Oh, won't you see?
   This gift He did endow!

I wish I could express in words
   His love for me, and how
He died for me to set me free!
   My sins I disavow!

I was the worst of sinners once
   Of anyone I know,
Yet He died for me upon that tree;
   My life to Him I owe!

I gave up on myself when there
   Was nowhere else to go.
He died for me to help me see
   How faith could daily grow!

The life that He has given me
   I never can repay.
He died for me! How can it be?
   The wonders of His Way!

There are much deeper feelings
   Which mere words cannot convey:
He died for me – that is the key
   That guides me every day!

(1981)
John 15:12-13

# Lies

"Sons of Satan," He exclaimed,
"You hypocrites and liars;"
"Who can save you," Jesus asked,
"From Hell's eternal fires?"

\*\*\*\*\*\*\*\*\*\*\*\*\*\*\*\*\*\*\*\*\*\*

Why does lying make Him mad?
Or when we break our word?
It only means that what I meant
Is not what you have heard!

So what! If I should tell a fib,
And hope that you'll believe?
Does it mean I'll go to Hell,
Or make somebody grieve?

\*\*\*\*\*\*\*\*\*\*\*\*\*\*\*\*\*\*\*\*\*\*

Liars so abuse the Truth,
They mock their only path
Of seeking faith that saves them,
And avoiding Godly wrath!

And what's a liar's witness
When he says that God is true?
Would his friends believe him?
Would he himself, or you?

(12/15/84)

# For Those Who Doubt

I've heard some claim that God is dead;
　That Jesus Christ exists no more!
But don't they know reality,
　And what on earth we're living for?

They love all Nature's wonderments:
　The swallow's flight, the waterfall!
They act as though they never thought
　That God Himself designed it all!

When wishful thinking is in vogue,
　Or bloated pride and self-esteem;
'Tis best to have a simple faith
　That grows beyond our wildest dream!

For if perchance they shall admit
　That life is more than hit-or-miss;
How Coincidence cannot explain
　Designs as intricate as this!

For if I were a gambling man,
　I'd cast my lot with He who saves,
Who beckons from the sheepfold's gate,
　And makes men rise from empty graves!

Faith then comes by hearing
　God's Word which we revere,*
And prayer will have the power, then
　To draw the Savior near!

And given but a moment's thought
  We might affirm it with a nod,
That the best our minds could e'er conceive
  Was put there by a loving God!

Convincing them is not my aim,
  (A time ago it was),
The reason why I must believe
  Is because – just because…!

Or better yet, if all was made
  Through Wisdom that is His,
Then living by His Rationale
  Is all the sense there is!

(3/30/88)
*Romans 10:17

# Judgment

Judge not lest ye be judged, they say;
        Though we cast our judgments every day!

Be careful if you make attacks;
        Judge only if you know the facts!

For God alone knows everything;
        Beware the arrows that you fling!

If to judge others you are driven:
        To the merciful is mercy given!

And if your judgment is begrudged,
        As you judge others, you'll be judged!

Christ died in order to atone,
        So, do not cast that angry stone!

We're fragile vessels made of clay;
        Think about it as you pray!

(9/19/09)
James 4-12

# The Son of God

Recall the blessed verses
    Remembered from our youth!
Acknowledge that our Holy God
    Would have us know the Truth!

For Jesus is the Lord of all,
    Dividing sheep from goats!
Our faith is not a tyranny
    Crammed down unwilling throats!

And evil works are not the way
    To earn divine reward;
But love is what we ought to give
    To neighbors, and our Lord!

He does not ask His followers
    To slaughter one another,
And make our world into a hell,
    With brother hating brother!

With mercy for the merciful,
    He shows us how to live;
And those who hate their fellow men,
    He teaches to forgive!

For Jesus died for all our sins,
    Our Hope when times are grim!
The gates of Heaven He holds wide
    To those who trust in Him.

(1/23/10)
John 14:6-7
Matthew 5:43-44

# The Holy Ghost

Some will deny, while others will insist;
We wonder, doubt, or sometimes we demur;
But does the Holy Ghost honestly exist?
Some believe, though others aren't so sure.

Is there a Spirit who will touch an empty heart
To help us sacrifice in love when we are called?
Is there a feeling that His Presence will impart?
What of those times when we were faithfully enthralled?

Do we explain those feelings just through Him,
Or as a nice emotion or a thought?
Then what explains the sweetness of a hymn?
It could be just a feeling, but it's not!

What brings us to the moments when we pray?
What moves our inner spirit to the uttermost?
What makes us ever willing to obey?
Could it really be the working of the Holy Ghost?

(6/2/81)
John 14:25-26

34

# Legacy of a Reformed Perfectionist

At times I feel like screaming
    When I'm always falling short!
My mind's assailed with bitterness,
    And doubts of every sort!

Who set my expectations
    So they always seem so high?
Must I strive to be a Christian?
    Will I struggle till I die?

Perfection in God's Kingdom Law
    In the Sermon on the Mount,
Makes odds against achieving it
    Impossible to count!

If answers are so absolute,
    What choices can we make?
And which of us can get through life
    Not making a mistake?

\*\*\*\*\*\*\*\*\*\*\*\*\*\*\*\*\*\*\*\*\*\*\*\*\*\*\*\*

We are not perfect creatures
    Because we often sin;
And since we rarely hit the mark,
    Alone, we cannot win!

Christ, Who dwells within us,
    Knows that we are frail;
And through His gracious mercy,
    He forgives us when we fail!

But one thing He has taught me,
    And I've found to be so true:
Forgiveness wasn't mine alone;
    It's meant for others too!

(5/14/81)

# Learning to Walk

So many miles I've paced upon the back porch overnight.
How many times I've worried that my pathway wasn't right.
I'd struggled with my conscience for so very many years,
Praying that the Lord would come and calm my lonely fears!

My wife and child departed from me early in the game;
I knew that on my own my life would never be the same.
I lived within a prison, but the Lord would comfort me.
I came to know that power which someday would set me free.

The years would come and go just like the buds upon the tree.
I tried to be the person that the Lord would have me be.
A wondrous hope He gave me, which isn't strange to some,
And the Truth within the Bible gave me strength to overcome!

He brought me to the point that I had long been waiting for:
To a certain understanding that I'd never felt before!
I used to think of all the things that I'd been striving toward,
But they fell along the wayside at the calling of the Lord!

That day I heard His knocking and I opened wide that door;
He entered in my heart as no one ever did before!*
He washed away the many sins, for which I was ashamed,
And showed me of forgiveness for the others that I blamed!

I think upon this mercy, which has come from up above.
My tears are now of joy about His faithfulness and love!
I'm seeking still direction, though He's pointing out the way.
No longer do I fear the trials that come to me each day.

If troubles seem to bring with them that old, familiar fear,
   They soon will vanish as I pray to bring the Savior near.
As I abide within His Word, He keeps me at His side,
   And His advice is always right; He is the perfect guide!

And even now, as I look back, I find it rather odd
   How a life of lonely pacing could become a walk with God!
For now it is enough to try to do the best I can
   To make the world a better place and help my fellow man!

(8/17/83)
Micah 6:8
*Rev. 3:20

# The Christian

I call myself a Christian,
    And hope that when I die,
My home will be in Heaven,
    Though at times I wonder; why?

What makes me so deserving
    That I'm worthy of His love?
Is my life so perfect
    That He'll call me up above?

As I look back upon my life,
    And think of all the shame,
For causing so much suffering,
    Yet Jesus took the blame!

I've lived with all His blessings,
    But forgotten what God's done.
He's called, but I've ignored Him,
    And the teachings of His Son!

He died for me, yet still He lives,
    So I can do so too!
I reap the blessings that He gives,
    Yet little do I do!

My life has been so "busy,"
    That I've failed to read His Word;
If faith then "comes by hearing,"
    Then too little I have heard!

Now, daily I shall find the time
　　To read His Holy Book!*
And with prayerful application,
　　Not elsewhere need I look!

I've heard from other people,
　　It won't matter where I start,
As I seek to find God's promises,
　　And write them on my heart!

　　And now, each time I think about
Our Savior on the Cross,
　　A wondrous Hope and Glory
Overcome my sense of loss!

And when others share our common faith,
　　My spirit gets a lift,
To see how many others, too,
　　Revere so great a gift!

For all the things God teaches me,
　　In gratitude I pray
That faithfully I'll put them
　　Into practice every day!

(4/20/09)
Psalm 19:9-11

# Sharing

Amongst the fear and trembling

    When I think God's work is done,

I find that doing what I ought

    Can be a source of fun!


And when I've done what in my heart

    Is absolutely right,

I try to share what I have learned

    Of Everlasting Light!


Nor can I claim the credit

    For this wondrous life anew;

I'd rather give the glory

    To the One to Whom it's due.

(11/10/11)
Matthew 5:14-16

# Universal Truth

Of countless planets in the skies,
    For reasons that were doubtless wise,
The Lord chose this, our Planet Earth,
    As home for His incarnate birth!

Do other creatures so diverse,
    Found throughout the Universe,
Accept the Lord as Savior too,
    And the Word of God as wholly true?

The day will come when we will see
    Why all of this was meant to be!
Glory then shall be supreme,
    And greater than a wondrous dream!

I'm sure our Father's Holy Plan
    Encompasses much more than Man;
And all that I'm required to do:
    Love God, and all our neighbors too!*

(7/12/10)
*Matthew 22:37-40

# Romans 12:9

Our God tells those who follow,
       "Love others as you should,"
But says that only hypocrites
       Love evil with the good!

His Word instructs believers
       That they ought to give some care
To the gift that they are given
       For discerning Truth from err.

It's important to remember:
       To attain our promised fate,
We love our God and neighbor, too,
       But evil we must hate!

And where we must make judgments,
       Love the sinners not the sins;
And if we can remember that,
       Then everybody wins!

(4/12/10)

# Who Belongs to Him?

Some will strive to please the Lord,
    While others are content;
Some are caught up in their sins,
    Though many will repent!

God loves His children, every one:
    The weak and the devout;
Those so full of spirit,
    And the others full of doubt.

For all His many followers,
    Now share a common goal,
Of gladly giving of themselves,
    Body, mind and soul!

And those who now belong to God
    Will love Him first and most;
Then love our neighbors as ourselves,
    And seek the Holy Ghost!

Then help your neighbors, friend and foe;
    Speak truth to them in love,
While asking God to share His Grace,
    And bless them from above!

For if you seek our Father God,
    You'll find He'll come to you,
So that daily, with His blessing,
    You can find a life anew!

(1981)

# Forgiveness

Life can be so pleasant,
    And much easier to live
When we forgive our brothers,
    And our brothers can forgive!

I know I must forgive as much
    As I'm forgiven too,
Nor can I hate a little bit,
    As others often do!

And I should love my enemies
    As much as I love friends,
Including other people
    Who will never make amends!

And when we seek forgiveness,
    We should offer it as well;
For our hating one another
    Is the shortest path to Hell!

I know I should be like a dove,
    And offer no offense,
And that caring for our neighbor
    Is the only common sense!

Lord, help us all to understand:
    We're blind until we see
How forgiveness for our brothers
    Can help to set us free!

(9/13/09)
Ephesians 4:32

# What Shall I Do?

What shall I do, Lord?
   What shall I do?
My woes are great,
   And my friends are few.

What shall I do, Lord?
   I hope You can hear,
And give me the courage
   To face my fear!

What shall I do, Lord?
   Why can't I see?
Is that Your kind voice
   That is calling to me?

What is the answer, Lord?
   Why am I blue?
Can I give up my life,
   And start following You?

Am I waiting for You, Lord,
   To give me a sign,
As daily I pray
   That the Savior is mine?

Is that then the answer, Lord,
   Deep in my heart,
That there's nothing on earth
   That can keep us apart?*

And how nothing can bring
   Me closer to You
Than by doing the deeds
   That You've asked me to do!

(8/24/09)
*Ro. 8:38-39
James 1:22-25

45

# In His Presence

What can I say to Thee?
　　Thy Grace and majesty
Fill all my being
　　With great awe and love!

Thy Presence humbles me;
　　Thou shall forever be
The answer to everything
　　I'm thinking of!

Thy Grace has rescued me;
　　Thy Love means All to me,
Thou, Lord of worlds, and
　　Heavens on high!

When I was lost and blind,
　　Crippled with troubled mind,
You offered hope and peace
　　As You drew nigh!

Joy fills my being now
　　As I remember how
Precious that moment was
　　When we did meet!

You lovingly saved my life
　　From all the endless strife,
Giving me faith to make
　　My hope complete!

Thou opened mine eyes to see
　　A wondrous Reality,
Where You'll forever be
　　None then too far!

In granting me Holy Peace,
　　You made the worry cease;
Now hopefulness can increase,
　　My Guiding Star!

# Transformation

I remember when my heart was cold,
    And hard as granite stone;
My "loved ones" I would often scold,
    And easily disown!

The only thing I felt was hate;
    I bore an angry rod.
I thought that I alone was great;
    I had no fear of God!

I never would apologize,
    For I was "always right!"
I thought that only I was wise;
    I always had to fight!

And then I lost my only mate;
    She couldn't persevere!
I found I wasn't quite as great
    As once it did appear!

I saw I reaped what I had sown,
    That I too was to blame;
The truth I wish that I had known
    Is:  life is not a game...!

Humbled, then, I made a prayer
    To the God Whom I'd ignored.
To Him my soul I'd finally bare,
    And forgive those I abhorred!

Then, in an unexpected act,
    He touched my anguished heart;
With love that hitherto I lacked,
    He gave me a new start!

Confessing, then, would set me free,
    And nothing could compare
With learning what I ought to be
    Through effort, faith and prayer!

Since then, my cup has overflowed
    With blessings from the Lord,
And priceless gifts that He bestowed
    From the bounty He has stored!

(11/25/11)<br>Romans 12:2

## Thundering Majesty

How bright the clouds flash in the night
  To show us signs of Heaven's might,
And rumbling thunder lets us know
  That God can conquer any foe!

The wind is roaring in the air,
  And trees are bending everywhere,
As if to show through sound and light
  That righteousness will win the fight!

Like standing at a big ship's prow,
  While storming waves lash o'er the bow;
The tempest sprays, yet you can tell
  Somehow, someway, that all is well!

It's good to see the storming strife;
  It livens up our daily life!
Windblown, grinning, we can say
  That God Almighty rules the day!

*(9/3/88)*

# Chapter 2 - Marriage & Divorce

In my first marriage, my young wife and I had many needs and expectations we looked to the other to fulfill. Neither of us had been equipped for this. When I returned from Southeast Asia, suffering from undiagnosed PTSD, my demands and unacceptable behavior increased; while at the same time, I seemed to have lost my ability to forgive or love either others or myself.

Though Christ "came into the world, not to condemn the world, but that the world might be saved through Him" (John 3:17), for years I found myself using the Bible as a weapon to criticize or condemn others, rather than for its wisdom and guidance in my own spiritual journey. It seems it took forever for me to realize that God's reproofs and admonitions were meant for me, too. Displaying true paranoia, whenever I thought I overheard others mention the words, "religious hypocrite," or "Pharisee," I always secretly and painfully felt that they were indirectly referring to me! Too often, they were!

All this served to drive my wife away during her own spiritual journey. After our divorce, she eventually discovered how to serve others in need by becoming a counselor to substance abusers. My own path led me to a new-found faith that marvelously met my deep, spiritual needs as it enriched my life beyond all expectations!

It was only later, during my second marriage, that I finally began to "walk the walk." 1 John 3:18 says it best: "Dear children, let us not love with words or tongue but with actions and in truth."

# In Truth...

Perhaps I've found the psyche's key:

I think its simple honesty!

It, better than the brewer's art

Unlocks the secrets of the heart,

And makes our thinking plain to see --

This attitude called honesty!

-- A cure for troubled soul and mind;

God's gift for all of Humankind!

When arguing brings out the gall,

And hatred causes us to brawl,

Pure truthfulness will often heal

The awfulness we think and feel.

For when we choose to make assaults,

It's hard to cast an angry stone,

If we forgive the other's faults,

And honestly confess our own!

(6/4/81)

# The Pearl

There's a story they tell of a beautiful pearl
That a Protestant boy gave his Catholic girl.
It was mounted in hope on a bright golden band,
And she wore it with pride on her delicate hand!

How true was their love now no one can say,
But they smiled so nice on their wedding day;
And many shed tears that spoke of their joy
For the Catholic girl and her Protestant boy.

And all went well and was generally great
But for prejudice, fear and a smidgen of hate!
So the seeds were planted to soon destroy
The love of the Catholic girl for her boy.

Then the Protestant boy discovered one day
That the heart of his lover was stolen away!
He cried in anguish and fought with his fears
That he'd seen the last of his happiest years!

They argued bitterly many a night,
And rare indeed was a lull in the fight!
Oh, where was the beauty once seen in the pearl
By the Protestant boy, and his Catholic girl?

But, before they embarked on their separate ways,
They remembered their God, and offered Him praise!
They thought of the pearl and its message of hope,
And prayed that the Lord would help them to cope!

There's a message herein for the couple who tries
To follow the pathway that's holy and wise;
For God wants His children to share in His joys,
For all His believers, the girls and the boys!

How marriage itself, from beginning to end,
Was meant to be shared with our life's greatest friend;
And how hope is abundant the more we're aware
That dreams were intended for couples to share!

For when those who would treasure a Pearl of Love
Have hearts that are truly born from above;
Then in sharing forgiveness and trust in the Lord,
Their lives can be blest and their faith restored!

(10/16/81)
1 Corinthians 13:1-7

# The Last Goodbye

We try to pick our mate with care,
But oftentimes our love is blind;
Though burdens we would gladly bear,
With loving heart and open mind!

And yet we lived in constant pain;
Why we fought I'll never know.
We argued if we'd wed in vain
To one who proved a bitter foe!

We never would apologize;
Which shortly turned the marriage stale!
Too soon I missed those dancing eyes
I'd seen beneath her wedding veil!

If marriage makes a man a king,
She forced me to defend my crown;
Our kingdom suffered everything:
Our building up; our tearing down!

I won't forget that final day,
Her doubting eyes, and silken hair;
Perhaps she felt a choice to stay
Would drive me deeper in despair!

"I had no right to hurt you…"
She cried in pain that final night;
Could it be compassion, then,
That made her want to end the fight?

Parting seemed so asinine,
The moment that we said goodbye;
I saw then she was never mine,
And part of me began to die!

Her spirit, which I'd loved before,
Now rent apart my troubled soul;
The bitterness we had in store
Soon would take its heavy toll!

(12/16/81)

# Letting Go

Never could I understand
What others seemed to know:
If you cannot save your marriage,
You may have to let it go.

Let go, then, of your other half,
But trust in God above;
You'll need His help in dealing with
The painful loss of love!

Let go of all your pet demands,
And let your children grow;
And as for aching memories,
- Just learn to "let it go!"

Let go of favors owed to you,
And go, then, with the flow;
Just make your goal survival…
As you practice letting go!

Give up the right to have your way,
And treasures that you keep;
And once you've swept your conscience clean,
Then get some needed sleep!

We enter life with nothing,
And with nothing we'll depart;
We must let go of earthly things,
Or they'll break our troubled heart!

(2006)
1 John 2:15-17
Matthew 6:19-21

# Realization

Back then I thought she got her kicks
    By playing fast and loose;
I used it to excuse the way
    I justified abuse.

She said we were a "mismatch;"
    In some ways she was right.
Like oil and water do not mix,
    We couldn't help but fight!

It took me nearly thirty years
    To see that I was wrong!
Our daughter had to point it out;
    Thank heaven she was strong!

I learned that hatred kills the soul
    Through failing to forgive;
It keeps us in a flaming hell
    In which we cannot live!

My "righteous indignation,"
    Behind which I would hide,
Was my excuse for arrogance,
    And unrelenting pride!

Today I see how totally
    In anger I was driven,
But nothing that she did to me
    Could not have been forgiven!

She raised a splendid daughter,
    And faced a world alone;
And showed courageous attributes,
    If the honest truth be known!

(10/27/11)
Ephesians 4:32

# Ruminations

After all is said and done,
I find I'm still alive;
And with the proper attitude,
I know I can survive!

For life is what we make it,
And we've no one else to blame,
If when we choose to break the rules,
We find we've lost the game!

Yet, love is like a present
Which can come to us each day
In quantities equivalent
To what we give away!

By sharing all the best in life,
And giving others hope,
We make our lives much easier,
And gather strength to cope!

And if we should by accident
Offend by what we say,
A simple, kind apology
Will brighten up the day!

So whether one's insightful,
Or with wit as sharp as knives,
Let's bring a bit of Heaven
Into everybody's lives!

(4/3/10)

# Love Poem II

Oh, how our lives could have been so different
   Had we learned to really love when we were young!
The many feelings we could have shared together,
   And the beautiful songs our hearts could have sung!

I haven't said how I loved your gentle embrace,
   Though I have . . . and all the little things about you
I now think of with warm affection when I'm alone;
   Moments as refreshing and gentle as the morning dew!

A quiet moment is all I need within my day
   To feel a smile grow within me, dreaming of us,
Thinking of the strength I've found from knowing you,
   The secret thoughts we once would quietly discuss.

Sometimes I have the feeling that as we live,
   Our lives were meant to be one . . . and intertwine;
A feeling much bigger than the both of us;
   That we may yet say: I am yours and you are mine!

(2006)

## The Christmas Gift

If I but had one gift to give

On Christmas day to you,

A theme I ever more wouldst live:

A love for you so true!


To offer you my heart, my love,

And never do you wrong;

To share our blessings from above,

And hear you sing a song…


For every melody you sing,

The angels would agree,

Sounds wonderful beyond compare!

And *marvelous* to me!

(12/25/2006)

# To Have and to Hold

Not too soon in my short life,
    I stumbled on the perfect wife!

When needed, she is always there
    To render each her loving care!

Her heart is blest with godly grace;
    And love is written in her face!

I love to stare into her eyes,
    Where faith's renewed and malice dies!

Our kisses, rare, but prized as gold,
    …No better one to have and hold!

Her spirit, ever free and fair
    Shows in her jeans and tousled hair!

Her genius is the very best
    On this side of eternal rest!

There's little that she doesn't know;
    Her intellect would seem to grow!

Forgiving, loyal, wise and kind,
    A better wife you'll never find!

Loving partner, steadfast friend;
    …True and faithful to the end!

(2006)

# Reconciliation

(Can be sung to the tune of Amazing Grace)

At times, before I pray to God,
    I want to call you first,
And right the wrongs I've done to you,
    Especially the worst!*

It's not enough that I regret
    Unwarranted abuse,
Or when I tried to cause you pain,
    -For that there's no excuse!

Indeed, there's nothing I can say
    To mitigate my shame;
I cannot justify myself
    For giving you the blame!

Please understand I'm willing now
    To walk the extra mile,
And do whatever it may take
    That we might reconcile!

I'm starting now to benefit,
    As I begin to learn,
That life is ever hopeful with
    Compassion and concern!

(11/1/11)
*Matthew 5:23-24

# Amends

Last night we had an argument;
  I don't remember why.
I'm sure if I thought long enough,
  I'd get it by and by.

Was it that important
  That we risked inflicting pain
Upon the one we love the most?
  It now seems so insane!

Three times today I called you,
  But the phone just rang and rang.
The thought you were ignoring me
  Gave my heart a pang!

How then can we communicate,
  And say the things we must;
And not condemn each other's thoughts,
  But be completely just?

We all can have our arguments,
  Provided we take care
To agree to follow ground rules,
  And insist on being fair!

I said you must support me,
  Or we might as well divorce;
Though you're best of all my critics,
  And it's wise to stay the course!

I've treasured your intelligence,
  And comments on my work;
And you've never failed to tell me
  When I'm acting like a jerk!

Alone, I often find myself
With feelings somewhat blue!
I'm willing now to make amends,
And apologize to you!

(4/11/10)

65

# Us

She is my wife, I love her, sir!
    The Lord chose me to care for her!

I find it isn't hard to see
    Our marriage troth was meant to be!

That day I asked her for her hand,
    On which I placed her wedding band,

The diamond that I chose to give
    Promised our new lives to live!

With two of us becoming one,
    We took our place beneath the sun!

To each we give the honor due,
    And celebrate our marriage true!

Together we have faced the world,
    As hopeful days about us swirled!

Life has proven true and just,
    The more we share our loving trust!

Yes, to care for her I'll do my best
    Until we find eternal rest!

(10/18/11)

# Nick and Marguerite

He always called her Marguerite;
   She loved to call him "Nink."
Her smile was so disarming,
   And he'd always grin and wink!

Three quarters of a century
   Their love held them together,
Through thick and thin, the ups and downs,
   With a bond as strong as leather!

Though seldom were they far apart,
   They could barely hear each other;
So they shouted out their pleasantries,
   From the one unto another!

So, Mom and Dad approached the end,
   Both barely skin and bone;
As God would have it, neither one
   Would have to go alone!

And so they meet their Maker,
   And before Him they shall stand;
Together, as they lived their lives,
   With loving hand in hand!

For long ago, Christ chose for them
   Their mansion in the sky;
Where she can smile forever,
   And see the twinkle in Nink's eye!

(5/02/10)
John 14:1-3 (KJV)

*Lily*

# Chapter 3 - To My Child

Shamefully, and with possessive jealousy, for many bitter years after our divorce, I tried constantly to drive a wedge between my ex-wife and our daughter; ostensibly to keep my daughter from "following in her mother's footsteps," but in actuality, to try to get revenge on my ex-wife and be number one in my daughter's heart. In due time, when my daughter saw through my thinly-veiled hatred; my efforts, of course, backfired, and only served to alienate her!

Much later, after I had grown up a little bit, in an effort to make amends in accordance with a 12-step program I was involved with, I sent conciliatory letters admitting to past, unacceptable behavior to both my daughter and her mother (my daughter called my letter "amazing!" and which she later said allowed for healing in her own life)! To my surprise, this also opened the door to a new understanding and relationship between her and me; and how in spite of all my previous, angry, self-righteous preaching at her, my daughter had discovered her own relationship with God, and she forgave me "from the heart," setting a good example for me to follow!

Now, we are getting to know and understand each other more with every passing day, achieving the true and loving relationship a father and daughter should have. Thank You, Lord!

## Morning Breezes

*Whispering among the trees*

*Are voices of the morning breeze;*

*Sometimes many, sometimes few. . .*

*Listen to them calling you!*


*Windblown branches, often loud,*

*Sound so like a roaring crowd;*

*Or other times might you agree,*

*It's like the surf beside the sea?*


*At times the wind will play a game:*

*Was it whispering your name?*

*Listen to the breeze someday;*

*The wind has many things to say!*

(1/10/83)

# Following

Never base your faith, my dear,
    On other people's love;
The love that counts the most, you'll find,
    Comes from up above!

For we are earthen vessels,
    Prone to sin and lie,
Some never knowing love and grace
    Until the day they die!

The best friends are believers,
    They're loyal, kind and true;
They know the One they follow,
    And will always welcome you!

# The Unicorn

As Xana sat upon the floor
  And watched the fire's embers;
Her thoughts were far beyond the door,
  Away from family members!

Then Xana left her father's knee,
  And ran to look outside;
Tonight, perhaps, she'd set it free;
  She hoped, but never tried.

The Unicorn was tied and bound
  Beyond the village square:
They kept it for its magic,
  But she thought it wasn't fair!

The beauty in its dignity,
  Its solitude and spirit
Drew Xana to the Unicorn,
  She loved just being near it!

Xana gently stroked its mane,
  Her resolution weak,
And as she loosed the iron chain,
  A tear ran down her cheek.

"Oh, Unicorn, I've set you free,
　　　Please hurry, you must fly!"
The Unicorn stood motionless
　　　Until he caught her eye!

For Xana had believed in things
　　　That some would never know;
And all 'twas found of either one
　　　Were footprints in the snow!

(1/18/83)

# The Flight of the Unicorn

At night they dance about the skies,
   And exercise their wings,
All creatures of the myths and tales
   And Unicorns and things!

And upon her noble Unicorn
   Young Xana loves to fly!
Watch for them and you may see
   Their streak across the sky!

They scamper through the Universe
   While living out their dreams;
To hide at times behind the moon,
   Or gather up its beams!

Exploring distant galaxies,
   And planets far and wide,
The Unicorn takes Xana
   On a fascinating ride!

Though Xana knows the creatures
   Of ancient tales and lore,
What she sees is nothing
   Like she's ever seen before!

Of all legendary animals,
   It's just the Unicorn
That has a special feature
   In the magic of its horn!

It makes the nicest dreams come true
   With a special touch of grace
That unlocks all the mysteries of
   Eternity and Space!

Forever will they share the joys
    Of prancing through the sky,
And those who never see them
    Are the ones who never try!

When the sky is black and cloudless,
    Look up into the night;
You can see the star they live on,
    It's the third one from the right!

(8/2/83)

# A Night to Remember

Darkness fell upon the town;
   The snow was crisp and deep.
Though Xana lay upon her bed,
   She couldn't go to sleep!

While staring out her window,
   Young Xana shed a tear;
She thought about her closest friend,
   And wished that he were near!

"Who believes in Unicorns?
   Or what they have to say?"
Echoed words that Xana heard
   Just the other day!

Who believed in Unicorns?
   Was she the only one?
Her faith had cost her many friends.
   Alas! She had but one!

So Xana waited for her friend,
   So much she hoped to learn!
She had so much to ask him,
   But when would he return?

For Unicorns are always free
   To prance the skies above;
And all that ever draws one near
   Is purity and love!

So Xana said her prayers that night
   With blessings for her guide,
And as she said "Amen" she heard
   Prancing hooves outside!

That night she rode the Unicorn
   Aloft the starry sky!
They talked of life and many things
   To make the time pass by!

Xana learned a lot that night
   Of honesty and truth;
And escaping all the pitfalls
   Of carelessness in youth!

How doing right, no matter what,
   Is always worth the cost;
For many do what isn't right,
   And many souls are lost!

The Unicorn brought Xana home
   With morning's early light;
A wiser, tired girl she was,
   After such a night!

Xana woke that morning
   When she heard her mother's call.
She sat up in her bed and asked,
Had she dreamed it all?

(12/13/83)

# Xana's Christmas

The day after Christmas was snowy but nice,
And Xana's best present was one without price;
The Unicorn left her these words of advice:

"Don't let your parents down;
   They brought you up.

"Be humble enough to obey;
   You may give orders someday!

"Choose your companions wisely;
   You become what they are!

"When the time comes,
   Choose only a date
     Who would make a good mate!

"Be master of your habits,
   Or they will master you!

"Always trust God,
   And do what He says;
     There is no better advice!

"Believe in yourself,
   Or no one else will either!

"Don't be afraid to do what's right;
   Keep your courage up,
     And it will keep you up!

"Don't let the crowd pressure you;
   Stand for something,
     Or you'll fall for anything!"

She reread his letter and stored it with care,
But his words in her heart would always be there.

(12/27/83)

## One Day While I Was Fishing...

I caught what I thought was a very big fish,
  But the hook stuck in his throat;
And when I tried to get it out,
  A whale jumped in my boat!

He was a very pretty whale,
  All blue and green and pink;
But he was just so very big,
  I thought that we would sink!

He turned around and scratched his head
  As though he had a hunch,
And looked at me and smiled and said,
  "I hope that you brought lunch."

"Mister Whale," I said real mad,
  You almost sank my boat!
With you and I both in here,
  She'll hardly stay afloat!"

"There must be one too many,"
  He said with an awful grin;
"Do you think that I should eat you?
  Or would you rather take a swim?"

I said, "But this is my boat!
  And I think you're very mean;
In fact, you are the rudest whale
  That I have ever seen!"

He said that he was sorry;
  He loved the give and take!
Then he smiled and bowed and shook my hand,
  And jumped back in the lake!

                                            Dad

# My Thunderbolt

I'm thinking of my younger days,
   When I was just a boy;
About those secret moments
   That would fill me so with joy!

How many times within our car
   I'd watch the fences rushing by;
And flashing near or swimming far
   Warm thoughts would blur before the eye!

One such thought would come to me:
   A horse;  I'd call him Thunderbolt!
A friend whom only I could see;
   Pure white, and gentle as a colt!

He ran beside us, so it seemed,
   Jumping fences, staying near;
For he was mine alone I dreamed;
   Those thoughts to me were very dear!

My Thunderbolt was there until
   I let him go when I was seven;
Invisible, and free at last,
   He'll be there when I get to Heaven!

(9/2/81)

# To My Child

There is a subtle trap, my dear,
        In doing as you please;
You think that you will own the world,
        And live a life of ease!

Though, with the best intentions,
        When we think our motives good,
Something keeps our lives
        From going smoothly as they should!

Yet dreams that we've imagined
        Are nothing quite so grand
As finding that Eternal Life
        That God Himself has planned!

Then Life's a wondrous challenge,
        And never are we bored,
As we grow in understanding,
        And our knowledge of the Lord!

So, do your level best, my child;
        He'll help you on your way!
Seek Him with an open heart,
        Every time you pray!

Draw closer to the Lord, my child,
        And He will come to thee,
With joyous meaning for your life;
        Try it and you'll see!

Always practice what you've learned,
        Every single day;
The rest you'll find out for yourself,
        As you travel on your way!

Love, Dad

# A Word to the Wise

If you give an inch to Satan, dear,
      He'll only take a mile!
Play his game of cheating,
      And you'll smile a crooked smile!

Give in to one temptation,
      And you'll find you've got them all!
The story is the oldest one
      Since Eve and Adam's Fall!

The Bible helps you see, my dear,
      How wrong is far from right;
How truth the Lord has spoken
      Can give you added might!

That strength you'll need in growing up
      In the coming years ahead,
In fighting off the Devil
      With Words our Lord has said!

Take up your shield and helmet, dear,
      Your sword and armor, too,*
Remembering those verses
      That the Bible taught to you!

Then Satan is no threat to you;
      You'll have him running scared;
But only if you're sure you've gone
      To battle well prepared!

(1/6/83)
*Eph. 6:10-18
James 4:7

# Verses

Debbie is a Christian girl,
       Or so she tells us all,
But ask her to recite a verse,
       And she forgets them all!

She never wrote her verses down;
       She never seemed to care,
But when she had a problem,
       She wept in her despair!

But Jenny learned her verses well,
       A new one every day!
She studies from the Bible
       Before she goes to play!

When things for her got difficult,
       A verse would come to mind.
She'd thank the Lord in Heaven
       For the answers that she'd find!

*********************************

So, if life presents a problem,
       The Lord can help us see,
As we recall His teachings:
       They're meant for you and me!

# Choosing a Mate

Decisions that you'll make, my dear,
    Are many and will vary,
But greatest is the one you'll make
    When you decide to marry!

I've tried to teach you many things
    While you were in your youth:
How trust is only possible
    When you honor truth!

The Word of God you'll find, my dear,
    Gives eyesight to the blind;
What joy to share the Lord with friends,
    No greater will you find!

Find the man whose God is yours,
    Who knows His Marriage Plan;*
To share your faith and love of life,
    As you go hand in hand!

Life is full of blessings
    For those who trust the Lord,
Honor God and you will find
    That life's its own reward!

The just shall live by faith, my child,
    Love with all your heart;
Find the man who does the same,
    And you will never part!

(1988)
*Eph. 5:21-33

# Chapter 4 - War

As an Air Force "brat," I was always interested in military matters. I applied for and attended the Air Force Academy to prepare myself to protect and defend my country and all that it stands for.

The result was not so glamorous. Our missions to bomb Asian "truck parks and ammo storage areas" in fact, ended up just bombing human beings! The dichotomy of following my conscience, "submitting oneself to the governing authorities" (Romans 13:1), and of "only following orders," as we had heard from many Nazi war criminals, was totally discomfiting to me! I had not yet managed to reconcile the deadly side of military duty in serving one's country with our obligations to the God who indeed commands us to love our enemies!

When I returned stateside, I was assigned to a SAC command post, where, in addition to being tasked to possibly launch both our nuclear bombers and missiles, we were issued side arms with orders to shoot any of our comrades who either failed to perform their duties, or who took unauthorized actions; which further contributed to the unabated stress that ultimately led to my psychotic breaks, and ended my marriage and career. It still impacts me to this day.

Only after decades of soul-searching did I imagine how it might be possible, as an alternative to war, to serve both God and country by maintaining peace through a sincere and active concern for the genuine needs and welfare of our fellow men around the world.

# Just the Facts

"War is hell," or so they say.
   A cause is bought; with lives we pay!
And we, as servants, set aside
   More personal desires,
To tend Hell's encompassing fires!
   Leaving fields of ashen ruin,
With rotting bodies stench perfumed.
   Quickly then our youth is past!
Our minds to bear this morbid scar!
   How long these times of hell will last?
Till our lives are spent in smoke and char?
   Or the flame put out by inspiration
From above,
   Disgust of waste. . .
     Or selfless love?

Ken White (1967)

## Identity Crisis

It's not that I'm averse to learning
  Inert facts to fill my mind!
It's not the knowledge that I'm spurning;
  To its virtue I'm not blind!
Math and Chem have found their place
  (Which no one will deny),
To help us win the Missile Race
  And build us jets to fly!
We didn't ask to fight a war
  For hills in Viet Nam;
But since we're in it, now we'll need
  A bigger, better bomb!
For wars are part of God's Design,
  Based on Nature's Laws,
And while I want to end the war. . .

  . . . I hope I'm not the cause!

(1969)

# Remembering Flanders Fields

In Flanders fields, still, poppies grow
As they once did long ago!
We know things now you never knew
That make us ponder as we view
Your crosses standing row on row
In Flanders fields!

Your Faith in Purpose, well instilled,
Suffered, once your blood was spilled;
Your war became none other than
The greatest slaughter known to man,
Whose noble aims were unfulfilled
In Flanders fields.

Your blazing torch, passed hand to hand,
Saw many battles, conflicts and
Throughout the years, in other wars,
Led more attacks on foreign shores
At a cost you'd surely understand,
In Flanders fields!

That flaming torch was ne'er so bright
As when you held it, grasping tight;
But once we dropped the final bomb,
We snuffed it out in Vietnam.
We learned so little from your fight
In Flanders fields!

Today that flame bursts forth anew,
As poppies in the springtime do,
Because of your impassioned plea,
We'll tend to Freedom's Destiny
And pay the debt we've owed to you,
In Flanders fields!

(1991)

# December 7th

How did they feel when they knew it was real?

    "Torpedo off the bow!"

The crowded skies, the upturned eyes,

    "Where did they come from, how?"

Like menacing flies in the darkening skies.

    A Sunday turned to hell!

The fires spread with hundreds dead!

    "Do your duty well!"


Bitter tears will last for years,

    But this day they would regret!

Down, not out, in the opening bout,

    The war's not over yet!

While tattered and torn, a spirit was born

    To avenge the honored dead!

We'd fight this war, like none before,

    With victory ahead!!!

(Dec. 7th, 1984)

90

# Bombing the Innocents

Bombs once fell on Coventry,
    And mighty Dresden, too;
But whether it was legal
    Depends on point of view!

Sacrificing innocents,
    And bathing them in gore
Is only tolerated
    As an act of total war!

But the killing of civilians,
    Just to hear them cry and scream,
Is an act of evil cowardice,
    And hate in the extreme!

Afraid to face a foe who's armed
    Is a common trait indeed,
Of those who slaughter innocents
    For their evil, mindless creed!

But worst of all are those who choose
    To brainwash little boys,
And teach them to kill others,
    Not to play with games and toys!

Decide, then, who your god is:
    The One who calls for Peace!
Or the one who incites hatred,
    And makes violence increase?

For the Lord, what e'er you call Him,
    Is worthy and He's Great,
But only if His message is –
    To love and not to hate!

(10/08/09)

# My First Bomb Run

'Twas night, at thirty thousand feet,
  With undercast below;
The moon, still high at midnight,
  Left everything aglow!

The last plane in a three-ship cell,
  We tunneled through the sky.
It seemed to be too nice a night
  For anyone to die!

The crew performed efficiently,
  Yet something was unreal:
My training taught me how to act,
  But how was I to feel?

It seemed so hard to reconcile,
  Amid the dream-like beauty,
All the things that I had learned
  Of justice, Faith and duty!

Who were these men beneath the clouds,
  Several miles below?
I felt the bomb doors opening, then,
  "Ten seconds left to go!"

This war within Cambodia
  Left some of us confused:
Because we flew on orders,
  Were we morally excused?

Things aren't always black and white;
    Sometimes they're simply grey!
With that, the bomber shuddered,
    And I stated, "Bombs Away!"

The clouds would flash beneath us
    As our bombs would hit the ground!
The crew was oddly quiet
    As we headed homeward bound!

* * * * * * * * * * * * * * * * *

My questions went unanswered;
    I think about them still!
That war made little sense to me;
    I doubt it ever will!

                                        Ken White

# Between Missions I

I spent the war in Thailand
      When the sun god would allow,
Lounging on my patio,
      Catching rays at U-Tapao!

While staring at my eyelids,
      I gripped my cola can,
And measured productivity
      By the color of my tan!

This time between the missions
      Was always such a bore,
For these were wasted moments
      In a very wasteful war!

(5/27/81)

# Between Missions II

I found it fascinating
    When the fighting was a bore,
To watch the mini-conflicts
    Upon my patio floor!

The ants would fight in combat there
    To claim another meal;
Some pulled east, the others west;
    Their diligence was real!

It was a simple tug-of-war;
    The prize was just a fly!
There was no honor here at stake,
    And no one had to die!

I lay there watching calmly,
    Dwelling on my thoughts,
Until the big invasion by
    The dreaded "nitnoy mots!" (little ants)

These little creatures had a goal
    That wasn't quite the same:
Not only did they want the fly,
    They liked to kill and maim!

The nitnoys swarmed around the fly,
    And stole it from the rest;
Then carved it up in little bits,
    And took it to their nest!

How many days I languished there
    To tally up the score,
And witness these grand strategies
    Upon the patio floor!

So, war taught me a lesson,
    One not to be forgot:
Go the victory and the spoils
    To the more determined mot!

# Remembering Vietnam
## (Cambodian Campaign)

No longer is it secret,
    Yet the facts aren't fully known
Of the war within Cambodia,
    Or the missions that were flown!

Wars are always tragic,
    But I feel that I must tell
About our heavy bomber crew,
    And our rendezvous with Hell!

Before our tour overseas,
    At first we had to train,
We eagerly went off to war;
    The waiting was a pain!

When our training was complete,
    We transferred then to Guam,
Where we prepared to meet the foe;
    Our weapon was the bomb!

This war against the communists
    Was one we COULD NOT lose!
We needed to eradicate
    The vicious Khmer Rouge!

So we ploughed up all the landscape,
    And bombed them in their beds;
We showed them righteous terror,
    Raining bombs upon their heads!

Between us stood five miles of air,
    A chasm cold and vast;
We knew not what went on below,
    Beyond the Plexiglas!

We joked we killed but monkeys
        In the forests' verdant trees;
In truth we slaughtered many men,
        To bring them to their knees!

The foe was painted evil,
        And anything but nice;
They warred upon their neighbors,
        And ought to pay the price!

They forfeited their right to live,
        For murdering our friends;
We'd make them taste our fury,
        Instead of make amends!

Our bombs were indiscriminate
        Within our target "box;"
Both innocent and guilty
        Fell before us bomber jocks!

But on one fated bomb run,
        Too early we did bomb;
We struck an allied rubber plant,
        And lost our cool aplomb!

We heard that many men were killed,
        Because of our mistake;
How wiping out our staunch allies,
        Was more than we could take!

To pacify our guilty thoughts,
        The staff convened a board,
And gave to us the accolade:
        "Outstanding Crew Award."

Their praise seemed so ironic,
  Our shame did not assuage,
Since we knew that we were guilty
  Of the Error of the Age!

Friend or foe we ne'er the less
  Snatched away their lives;
We made them into memories
  Of neighbors, kids and wives!

How many did we maim or kill,
  To turn the quick to dead?
For we were more effective
  Than a bullet to the head!

But is it right to take a life
  When commanded not to kill,
By a power even higher
  Than you'll find on Capitol Hill?

We came back home as heroes,
  To Hades we had been;
I had this nagging, ugly thought
  That all we'd done was sin!

We got our share of medals,
  But somewhere in a hut,
A mother, wife and children
  Felt anguish in their gut!

I couldn't think of other things,
  But was haunted in my head,
By the mournful, everlasting cry,
  And chanting of the dead!

We must keep war a tragedy,
    - A cause for deep regret;
Which hopefully will make us ill,
    In case we should forget!

So, if again we're tempted
    To engage in pointless strife,
We honestly must ask ourselves
    If it's worth a single life!

Our purpose must be worthy,
    So those who have to fight
Will never have to question
    If what they did was right!

For when we do the duty that
    Could ask the highest price,
Let it be for noble reasons,
    And well-worth the sacrifice!

Let Freedom be the only cause
    That justifies a war;
For never should we be in doubt
    Of what we're fighting for!

Let's honor everyone who served
    And give them each their due!
Saluting their courageous fight
    For God and country, too!

(4/06/09)

# A Dying Breed

Oh, once there was a bomber jock
   Who tread the halls above;
His job he found was duty-bound,
   With very little love!

He was, each time he had to fly,
   Overwhelmed with dread
For everyone he'd caused to die,
   And the blood upon his head!

He knew the war was fighting for
   A world of love and peace;
But after years of toil and tears,
   He wished that it would cease!

Though often told that he was bold,
   He knew that deep inside
His troubled heart was torn apart,
   And his hope had all but died!

He'd served so well in times of hell
   But his conscience nagged him still;
The truth was tough: he'd had enough,
   And no more could he kill!

With some remorse, he tried, of course,
   But found no cause to brag;
So, without recourse, he left the force,
   No more to serve the flag.

His former friends made no amends,
   Which he could ill afford,
For it added to his worries
   As he paced the psycho ward!

He saw the world full of hate,
   And so he chose to see
His dreams of love and honor
   As the true reality!

He was sick of diagnoses,
   Of neuroses and psychoses,
For his intellect was dying
   On the vine!

With his tenderest emotion
   For the nurse who rubbed in lotion,
What had happened to his thinking
   Was a crime!

Despite the writing on the wall,
   He saw some meaning in it all,
While others saw him wasting
   In the past.

They bet he'd be a goner
   If he kept his code of honor,
So they undermined his ego
   To the last!

And even yet today,
   We understand he's going to stay
On the ward, behind that door –
   Just another vet the world can ignore!

(11/27/81)
Galatians 5:14-15

# The Final War

When Russia launched the first strike
    It caught us unawares.
It looked as though the score would be
    In favor of the Bears!

We kept our missiles in the ground,
    Trusting in our hopes
That it was just some flights of geese
    Seen on our radarscopes!

The bombers were launched quickly.
    The crews had lots of drive;
That's because they thought they'd be
    The last ones left alive!

So we'd withhold our missiles,
    Sending bombers in alone
To face the greatest air defense
    The world had ever known!

Our subs moved to position
    To help us change the score.
The Russ would really pay the price
    (If not too far from shore!)

Back home with little time left,
    We were running to and fro',
Asking others what to do,
    But no one seemed to know!

The radio announcer said
    That we should persevere,
And store up water, food and clothes
    To last at least a year!

"Now they tell us," so I said,
    "I'd really like to know
How we'll gather what we'll need
    With minutes left to go."

Some were breaking into stores,
    Stealing goods and cash.
They weren't aware that soon they'd be
    Thermonuclear ash!

Many heard the sirens
    When attack was imminent,
But went about their business,
    Not knowing what it meant.

Our Plan against the Russians
    On which our strategy was built
Was once they'd blown us all away,
    Perhaps they'd die of guilt!

Our public was their "hostage,"
    That's what our War Plan said.
I wished we had more choices left
    Than "Better dead than Red!"

We'd built up our deterrence
    So that peace alone made sense,
But one thing that we'd overlooked
    Was national <u>defense</u>!

Realistic thinking wasn't
    What our Plan entailed,
No one had considered that
    Deterrence might have failed!

Gambling all that's dear to us,
    Is an unamusing twist
To a military doctrine
    Based on "Calculated Risk."

Victory in the aftermath
    Is for those left alive,
We knew that we would buy the farm,
    But they planned to survive!

The Russ, who'd trained their populace,
    Had factories underground:
They knew they'd be protected
    When our missiles were inbound!

By showing them our willingness
    To sacrifice it all,
We hoped they wouldn't nuke us
    With our backs against the wall!

Civil Defense was the issue,
    Since survival was the crux,
But a Federal Program can't be run
    On twenty thousand bucks!

About our Civil Strategy,
    I think our leaders lied:
They said that with Deterrence,
    You don't need a place to hide!

Then some would say, "The American Way
    Is await a war's arrival
Before saying 'Shucks' and paying bucks
    For national survival."

The end came rather suddenly,
    - No time to get the jitters.
With a shock wave and a brilliant flash,
    We were crispy critters!

Those with fallout shelters,
    Who'd heard the first alert,
Became the heirs to this new land
    Of radioactive dirt!

Our missiles, which had been withheld,
    Much as you'd expect,
Sustained a multitude of hits,
    And most of them direct!

Since we had no missiles left,
    They deftly won the war,
By threatening that they'd do again
    What they'd just done before!

The terms were harsh and crystal clear,
    So there'd be no mistake:
Surrender or be vaporized,
    Was our choice to make!

You might say that our strategy
    Was just a trifle crude!
I hoped the one's who'd thought it up
    Were justly barbecued!

We'd been told war wouldn't happen…
    They called it "tommyrot,"
But for many was this epitaph:
    "The Unthinkable was thought!"

We wonder of the remnant
    That the war had left behind;
Now the noble task before them
    Is but renewing of the Mind!

The Final War: Morals

The strength of our Deterrence
    Depends on how it is perceived.
But it loses its effect
    When it's simply not believed!

The concept of Deterrence
    Very soon becomes a farce
When Russians think assured destruction
    Will not be theirs, but ours!

The Soviets think differently
    About the war we dread:
That it isn't just the war that counts,
    But who comes out "ahead!"

If you think that nuclear fireballs
    Will bring about some tears…
The effects of biochemicals
    Will last for many years!

Victory in a nuclear war,
    As many will discover,
Depends less on the missile crews
    Than those who must recover!

I'd like to see a boxer
    Who made it through first round
By simply throwing punches
    While his guard was always down.

When defense policies are made,
    They shouldn't be neglecting
To have some small provision for
    Those they are protecting!

I have this mental image
    Which to me is quite profound:
Of soldiers marching off to war,
    While the fort burns to the ground!

All the major issues
    That our nation faced before
Are paled to insignificance
    By a thermonuclear war!

(1981)

# The Real War

We have no trenches in our war,
    We're not bombarded through the night;
But we know what we're fighting for,
    And that our cause is always right!

Our weapons, though not made of steel,
    Are better suited for our needs;
This war is fought more subtly,
    With thoughts and words and deeds!

This greatest war is waged unseen,
    In darkness bright as day;
Yet just living as we ought to
    Keeps the enemy at bay!

When others lack the means whereby
    To wage a winning fight,
Just let them know the origin
    Of Everlasting Light!

For we can fight with confidence
    In something that we know:
The battles fought today were won
    Two thousand years ago!

(1968)
Eph. 6:12

# La Croix

A medal of another war,

   Fought many years ago,

Lay rusted on a rain-soaked plain,

   Beneath the crusted snow...


Who knows what glory had it then?

   Or laurels to the brave?

Now, its owner and his honored tale

   Lie hidden in a grave!


Ken White (1968)

# Epitaph

On Earth or above,
There is no greater love
Than to lay down one's life for a buddy;
And many a story
Of honor and glory
Ends with a hero so bloody!

From our cities and farms,
Our boys took up arms,
That our nation may always be free;
So we live out our lives,
And each of us thrives,
Since our youth died for you and for me!

For precious are those
Who honorably chose
To meet with annihilation;
They laid down their lives
For their children and wives,
And the deep gratitude of their nation!

In our troops we take pride,
Those who live and who died;
They gave of themselves for their cause;
We honor them now,
And their praise we avow,
For their courage gives moment to pause!

There's no reason for sorrow,
Today or tomorrow;
They sacrificed that we should live
To meet with our foe, and share what we know
Of the joy that comes when we forgive!

(8/1/10)
John 15:12-13

# Chapter 5 - Just for Fun

Humor can be our last defense against insanity. I have always tried to see the humorous side of any situation. Given my experiences and condition, I've needed to!

During many difficult, grim, or intolerable periods of my life, I have resorted to my own particular (some say peculiar) brand of humor to get through them. Whether it's using zany antics in high school plays, to speaking Russian to my Academy art instructor (who was convinced I was a Soviet "sleeper"), to putting a sprinkler inside the kitchen door of the neighborhood grouch, and turning the water on, it has all been Just For Fun!

I continue to invoke humor whenever possible, drawing upon our anthropomorphic cats, political situations far too ridiculous for words, or the usual foibles of basic human behavior, including my own! If we don't take ourselves too seriously, life offers constant and ongoing material.

Once, when visiting me, my daughter took me to see *Braveheart*, during which I was horrified in thinking that, in the making of the film, the actors had actually killed themselves simply for my entertainment! Subsequently, whenever I would tell my wife that I felt so logical and "normal" that perhaps I might never have been ill to begin with, she invariably responds by saying only one word: *"Braveheart!"* – to which I could only smile and say, *"Touché!"*

*Dulcibella*

# Dulcibella

There is a tale they often tell
  Of temperamental Dulcibelle;
A cat of many colors, she,
  Street-wise, unfettered, ever free!

…Often feared by one and all;
  She laid the rule by tooth and claw;
Every time she fussed or fought,
  She always gave more than she got!

But if you scratch her ears and chin,
  It seems she'd give a kitty grin;
And sweetly she might take a nap
  So gently then upon your lap!

So tell her that she's sweet and pretty,
  And she becomes the nicest kitty!
So do not judge an angry cat…
  But give her head a loving pat!

(8/27/11)

*Sam*

# Sam

Sam's a very loving cat,
  But rarely does he purr.
He always slinks around the house;
  A fluffy ball of fur!

He sits upon the windowsill,
  Surveys his wide domain,
Then leaps upon your sleeping chest,
  Causing ample pain!

He wakes you up at breaking dawn,
  When morning comes anew,
So you can scratch the fuzzy back
  Of none but you-know-who!

He loves to play with other cats;
  He wouldn't hurt a fly.
If ever there was cause to fight,
  He wouldn't even try!

For Sammy knows that he's the king,
  The lord of all he sees.
He knows full well who's number one,
  So, bow, then, if you please!

(9/24/11)

# Catnip

What makes a kitty do a dance?
      Another do a flip?
It's something they go wild about…
      A little pinch of "nip!"

What makes a kitty grab your arm,
      And hold it in his grip?
Which makes a cat go crazy,
      But a little pile of "nip!"

What will make a kitty
      Jump, stumble, sprint and trip…
That strange and wondrous powder
      Which is known as kitty "nip."

What makes a cat go bonkers,
      And leap to be alive,
And is a perfect reason
      Why kitties shouldn't drive!

(9/24/11)

# A Night at the Opera

Boo-boo Bear and Pooka Biddy*
    Went to an opera in the city,
Where sang soprano Lily Fish,
    Who among the cats was quite a dish!

With lovely alto, Dulcibella,
    - The dream of many a feline fella;
They sang their hearts out all the night,
    Their stars had never shown so bright!

A chorus sang for all to hear
    The best rendition of the year!
The supporting cast had stars so big
    As Elmo, Sam, and the Great Fizzgig!

Ovations of the feline crowd
    Brought encores lustily meowed;
No sooner was the opera past,
    They joined a party for the cast.

Before them they found treats galore,
    Like "nip" and toys worth waiting for!
Then Boo-boo, Pooks, and the stars who sang
    Ate chicken mousse and a fish meringue!

(9/24/11)
*Rocky and Sparky

# Fizzgig Hits the Mark

Our latest family member,
        (Fizzgig is his name),
Was raised within a bathroom
        Where he earned his share of fame!

The dogs would run the household,
        But they feared the kitty's claws,
So the cat stayed in the bathroom,
        In accord with family laws!

To give them all a happy life,
        Fizz thought that he should move.
When Mommy brought him north with her,
        He quickly found his groove!

It seemed that when we'd brush our teeth,
        Or wash our hands and face,
The Fizz would sprint ahead of us,
        And take his honored place.

He'd spring up on the royal throne
        Whene'er he felt the urge;
And sitting by its open hole,
        He'd balance on the verge.

And as we shut the faucet off,
        When finished with the sink,
We heard a steady tinkling noise,
        Which made us stop and think!

So Fizzgig did what people do,
      And played the human role,
As carefully he took his aim
      Into the toilet bowl!

When finished, he would leave the room;
      No more compelled to rush;
Now all we have to teach him is:
      The proper way to flush!

(5/15/11)

# Fizzgig's Reign of Terror

All hail the mighty Fizzgig,
    A garland for his head,
Reach out and try to hold him,
    And he'd rather run instead.

For Fizzgig torments all the cats,
    Though kitten he may be;
Jet-black and full of mischief,
    And cute as all can see!

We know his favorite tactic
    Is quickly hit and run,
Or launch into a scratching war,
    Although it's all in fun!

The other cats are wary –
    He's much too wild for words;
They think his kitty antics
    Are strictly for the birds!

He runs and jumps o'er Rocky,
    Each plot on Sparky fails;
Though Sam and Dulcie glower,
    He rarely shows his nails.

He pokes his brother Elmo,
    And bothers tiny Lil,
He aggravates poor Nigel;
    At times they're fit to kill!

He perches on the windowsill,
    And scampers down the hall;
He hides beneath the dresser,
    And swats at one and all!

We see how much he trusts us
    While curled up in our laps.
Few sights are quite as pleasant
    As Fizzgig taking naps!

(3/12/11)

# The Voters' Choice

My enemies say I'm too sick
To grace the body politic;
They say I couldn't win the race,
Because I'd be a "big disgrace!"

There's no way I can help the poor
As long as we must fight the war;
I proudly withheld veterans' pay,
Until the budget went my way!

Our deficit and debt have grown,
So I've chopped welfare to the bone;
And spending for defense I've cut,
To cinch the belt around our gut!

I humbly keep our proud flag furled,
While seeking to disarm the world;
Today, our nation can't be had,
(Unless attacked by Trinidad!)

Thru' policies that I had made,
We've given China favored trade,
They undersell what we once sold,
They'll own the world before we're old!

And since I always aim to please,
Our labor force is overseas;
I hope our workers can survive,
And foreigners can learn to thrive!

When others' faith would want us dead,
I won't abide the threats they've said;
We found we can avoid the fights
By forfeiting our basic rights!

Too few would seem to buy my pitch
To overtax the poor, not rich;
For congressmen need pork and graft,
And bucks to keep them overstaffed.

My voting record makes me proud,
Tho' campaign promises I vowed
Could not be kept; at any rate,
I think it's due to Karmic fate!

Don't say that I'm a mental case,
To want to settle outer space;
My faith asserts each man and wife
Will populate a globe with life!

Remember, friend, and be advised,
To always be aware of lies;
So, vote your choice; you could do worse,
(But guard your wallet, watch your purse!)

(5/18/12)

*Fizzgig*

# Chapter 6 - Potpourri

Poets need to be lovers of words. Thankfully, all through school, vocabulary words were a big part of English class. These words were often chosen evidently at random with no apparent congruity or theme. Putting them together in a single work whether prose or poetry was always an ongoing and enjoyable challenge.

Some of these efforts of mine at the Air Force Academy Preparatory School were predecessors to my current work, but in such primitive form that they barely warrant the title "poetry," and certainly fall short of the mark for humor. Perhaps the least repulsive of the surviving examples of my work is as follows:

> Oh God, here comes the <u>harlequin</u>
> To plague us with his spirit!
> Please notify my next-of-kin;
> I fear I'll die to hear it!

Potpourri, indeed!

# The Choice

The issue isn't WHO will thrive,
   Or swell the unemployment rolls;
But will our nation yet survive,
   So *anyone* can reach their goals?

For many years, we've clearly known,
   Tho' Special Interests fight us yet,
To regain surplus that we've blown,
   We must find ways to cut the debt!

There may be time to change our fate
   If we invest in teachers' pay,
To whet the skills that made us great,
   So once again we'll lead the way!

Whatever kinds of lives we live,
   Though we be very rich or poor,
It's not to get, but what we give,
   That is the goal worth striving for!

For we can reach our hopes and dreams
   As long as it is understood:
That we must share our gifts and skills
   To benefit the *common good*!

So help our children to succeed,
   To solve the problems we could not,
By giving them the tools they'll need,
   In the finest schools that can be sought!

(9/22/12)

# Freedom of Speech

Courtesy does not intend
        To say the things that might offend,
But our support will never cease
        For others' right to speak their peace!

How else may we have dialogue –
        And find the truth, amid the fog;
To hear from others and discern
        New thoughts that help us grow and learn?

If others don't like what they hear,
        They shouldn't offer cause to fear,
But pray that God will then bestow
        The wisdom that they need to know!

And if you doubt the point of view
        Or thoughts that others think are true;
Remember, though, when you correct,
        Be sure to do it with respect!

So if engaging in debate,
        We must be careful not to hate;
But be as harmless as a dove,
        Exemplifying brother love!

For precious is our right to speak;
        To praise or otherwise critique,
Without the fear of being jailed,
        Or having all our lives curtailed!

(9/24/12)

# Some Needs

You have to have the courage to lead an honest life!
    You'll need to find endurance to overcome the strife.
You'll have to have some honor to find what's right and true.
    And more than any other – the faith to see you through!

You'll need a lot of courage to find what's really best.
    Endurance will enable you to finish every test,
And honor will in glory keep your word as good as gold,
    While faith in times of trouble will help you to be bold.

Courage gives the fortitude to walk the extra mile,
    And one must have endurance to face each daily trial!
Honor means your promises you always mean to keep,
    And faith – the trust you have in God before you go to sleep!

How do you find the courage to face another day?
    From where will come endurance to see you on your way?
What is the source of honor that always is so right?
    Or faith that gives assurance of a future pure and bright?

That courage comes from failure and the faith to grow anew!
    Endurance means to persevere until the job is through!
Honor comes from suffering the pain of being wrong!
    And faith – from trusting God, however hard, however long!

(6/23/83)

# Freedom Isn't Free

On the front door of some neighbors
    Is a flag for all to see,
And beneath it is a motto
    Saying, "Freedom Isn't Free."

It's not just evil terrorists,
    Against whom we should preach;
We must beware when others care
    So little for free speech!

Don't fear to censure evil,
    Or the hatefulness it's from,
Nor shun the act of speaking out,
    For fear of what might come!

It isn't wisdom that we share,
    But hatred, pure and blind,
To excuse the evildoer,
    Or the scheming of his mind!

Our rights must all be exercised,
    Or else they shall be lost,
And we'd all be left to suffer
    At a terrifying cost!

For God bestows our Freedoms,
    And men died to help us see
The truth in that expression:
    That "Freedom Isn't Free!"

(4/11/10)
Galatians 5:1

# Behold, The Sparrow!

Christ saw things we seldom see,
As He walked the paths of Galilee!
His thoughts transcended daily strife;
He spoke about Eternal Life!
Comparing us to flighty birds,
There is a wisdom in His words.
Rarely is the sparrow hurried,
The future leaves him quite unworried.
God watches over sparrows, too,
So won't you let Him care for you?

# The Waging of Peace

Our Freedoms and our basic rights
Were gained through many bitter fights,
And we would suffer deep despair
If they were lost through lack of care!

We ought to be prepared, of course,
To guard our rights with measured force;
Though progress only comes, it seems,
By sharing peaceful hopes and dreams!

For history is replete with war,
And causes not worth fighting for;
While myriads of men were slain,
Whose lives were forfeited in vain!

Rather we should set our sights
On helping others gain their rights;
So they may also then rejoice
In learning how to use their choice!

So, blest are those who seek the peace,
And try to make the conflicts cease,
Who overcome their fears, and dare
To show their neighbors love and care!

For enemies could be our friends,
If we'd confer and make amends,
So we can live in peace with others,
Learning that we're truly brothers!

(9/22/12)
Matthew 5:9

131

# When I Was Young

When I was young, I used to feel
    Out of step and set apart!
When others spoke with confidence,
    Dark envy filled my heart.

I often wished that I were they,
    It clouded my emotions!
Others seemed to live their lives,
    While I went through the motions!

To see a smile when I had none,
    Such joys in me were missing,
Would I ever know, I asked,
    Of laughter, mirth, and kissing?

I often wondered what went on
    In another person's head;
Why were some so full of joy,
    And others full of dread?

So much of life, when I was young,
    Remained misunderstood.
I wondered when I'd learn myself
    Of telling bad from good!

And who I'd be when I grew up?
    - Would often cross my mind,
And in a mirror ten years hence,
    Who there would I find?

Now I'm the one who years ago
    Had wondered who would be,
And all the thoughts I struggled with,
    Are now just part of me!

Wondering is the stuff of Life,
    - The essence of our being,
And many dreams I'd hoped to see
    Are now what I am seeing!

# Breaking the Curse

I ran across a fellow once
  Who always used to swear;
He thought that all his cursing
  Gave his speech a little flair!
At any rate he wrongly thought
  That others wouldn't care.
For me, I found his talk
  Almost impossible to bear!

You're judged by every careless word
  You utter every day!
You're known less for your actions
  Than the words you choose to say.
For what you've hidden in your heart
  Your speech will soon betray;
Whether thoughtfulness or ugliness,
  It works the same each way!

So when you speak do try to have
  A little self-control!
Make eloquence and clarity
  Your purpose and your goal!
Instead of using words that shock,
  Choose speech that will console;
You'll find that cordiality
  Does wonders for the soul!

(1981)

# PTSD

Some soldiers don't receive a quarter
    For Post Traumatic Stress Disorder!
The ones you'd think have seen a ghost,
    May have a case, undiagnosed!

An unrelenting war they wage,
    While lashing out in mindless rage!
You take it out upon your mate,
    While harboring a vicious hate!

You cannot seem to hold a job;
    Life becomes a *danse macabre!*
Each day is filled with bitter strife;
    You can't find meaning in your life.

The future hasn't much in store…
    …But memories about the war!
With implications of disgrace,
    The past is difficult to face!

It's sometimes hard to find a friend
    On whom you always can depend;
Nor does it help to be annoyed,
    Each time that you're called paranoid!

It's always tempting to get high,
    Or end the struggle not to die!
So help your friends to understand:
    At times you need their guiding hand!

Regretfully, you're seldom blind
    To what has happened to your mind,
As ugly, evil thoughts intrude
    To put you in a fearful mood!

You find that ever since the war,
    You don't know what you're fighting for;
But there's a feeling deep inside
    Of anger that you cannot hide!

Each day you find a way to cope…
    …May be your only source of hope!
Yet, haunted by the horrid dreams,
    You can't ignore those anguished screams!

At last, your doctors come to see
    How you could have PTSD,
And after taking an exam,
    You get some help from Uncle Sam!

Though, if your illness is full-blown,
    You cannot treat it on your own;
But when you're given expert care,
    New hope replaces dark despair!

You get your meds and therapy,
    And things improve, though gradually,
But take these words of mine to heart:
    It falls on you to do your part!

I find this is a worthy fight,
    (Though still at times I'm not quite right),
But you will find your hopes have grown,
    As you perceive . . . you're not alone!

(2/24/12)

# Sparky

Sparky is our largest cat.
    He thinks he's human, too.
An orange, longhaired Tabby,
    And the smartest of the crew!

He thinks we live to feed him.
    He always loves to dine,
He knows he is our equal,
    And an epicure so fine!

He salutes us with an upturned tail,
    As he strolls across the room.
Ask if he's "hungweestarving"
    And he's ready to consume!

He wakes up when we're sleeping,
    And bites our toes and heels
To tell us that he's ready then
    To start his daily meals!

He finishes his mealtime
    With one of his patrols
Eating food that might remain
    In the other kitties' bowls!

He smiles that kitty grin of his –
    A cute, inverted frown,
And plays with you his favorite game
    Of staring people down!

We never drop a hint to him
    We think he's getting fat.
It helps when he walks on our backs --
    Our chiropractor cat!

At night he sometimes caterwauls
    To his rubber orca whale!
He's loudest when we try to sleep,
    As we listen to his wail!

A family member Sparky is,
    A good friend, true, and old,
For all the trips made to the vet,
    He's worth his weight in gold!

So cats have personalities
    For which they are adored!
The folks they own have always known:
    They are Heaven's sweet reward!

(9/1/09)

# Bart

I often used to wonder why
    My wife would always start to cry
At mention of a cat named Bart,
    Who evidently owned her heart!

For she and Bart though two were one;
    Together they would have great fun.
Whenever she would leave their house,
    He'd play with toys or catnip mouse.

With brother Sparky, Bart would play,
    And chase each other all the day.
When in the tub my wife would rest,
    Bart gently laid across her chest.

And when she'd move beneath her sheet,
    Young Bart attacked her legs and feet,
And did the things cat-lovers know
    That cause us to adore them so!

For Bart was brilliant for a cat,
    And thrilled to get a loving pat;
With magic he would nurse her ills,
    And cure her when she got the chills.

She couldn't help but think that Bart
    And she would never be apart;
But Fate's a thing without a head,
    And we must go where it has led.

She'll always rue that fateful day
    A mosquito bit him while at play.
However much she loved her Bart,
    She couldn't cure his crippled heart!

By accident she had to stay
    At home on that regretful day,
And held her Bart against her breast,
    As he passed on to blessed rest!

But never can there be an end,
    When one would have so great a friend;
And we shall take our comfort then
    In knowing we shall meet again!

                    Ken White (3/19/12)


*~ For Bart ~*

*Though nothing can take away the pain of losing a loved one, greater still is the joy and love you get from those you rescue and take into your life. I encourage everyone looking for a new and loving friend to check animal shelters, rescues, such as Rikki's Refuge, or ferals, for those who need and want you as much as you do them. You will never regret it!*

                    *Marcia*

# Rocky (The Prodigal Cat)

We have a cat named Rocky
    Who deeply touched my heart;
And since we first acquired him,
    We'd never been apart.

I've seldom felt a pain as deep
    As when he ran away;
I felt it was my fault he left
    On that remorseful day!

Perhaps I was distracted
    When he snuck out through the door
An act of total stealthiness
    He'd never done before!

My heart so ached with longing
    When I found that he had left.
The thought of him a lost, stray cat
    Left me grieving and bereft.

I searched throughout the neighborhood
    While calling out his name.
It seemed to be to no avail;
    I knew I was to blame!

The cold would soak my clothing;
    But a vigil I would keep;
And wait forever, if I must
    And forego any sleep!

Hours came and slowly went,
    I peered along the street.
I thought that Rocky might return
    To warm his little feet.

How many prayers I said that night
    That Rocky might come home,
If not, I feared him hurt or lost,
    Or evermore to roam!

At last, my prayers were answered!
    He came strolling up the walk;
I was so thrilled to see him,
    I could barely even talk!

He eyed me somewhat quizzically,
    (He'd not been gone for long);
And he wondered what, if anything,
    Could possibly be wrong!

I cuddled him within my arms;
    His eyes stared deep in mine!
I've rarely had a moment
    So exquisitely divine!

But I saw lurking mischief
    In his wide and sparkling eyes:
His little act of innocence
    Was merely a disguise!

He sauntered back into the house,
    And winked as if to say
To all his new-found friends outside:
    "...Be back within a day!"

Ken White (3/20/09)

# The Gift

When Uncle John stopped writing me
    About a month ago,
I knew he had a problem;
    What it was, I didn't know

John always sent me letters
    I've treasured since my youth!
In each I'd find an element
    Of universal truth!

His writing brought me laughter,
    And overcame my fears;
In some I found such tenderness
    That I was moved to tears!

I always loved to read his verse,
    And essays that he'd write;
And digging through his archives
    Always filled me with delight!

I was a special fan of his,
    While he was fond of me;
And all the wondrous things of life
    He taught me how to see!

He could have been the author
    Of many famous books,
But he filed away his manuscripts
    In crannies and in nooks!

John's family hadn't known him;
    He was seldom understood.
They thought nothing was of value
    Unless it earned a livelihood!

Whenever brilliant insights
    Would come to John in thought,
He'd put them down on paper,
    Lest they'd be forgot!

I'd driven miles to see his files
 From my own home far away;
For I got John's funeral notice
 Only just the other day!

John's house looked cold and empty
 When I came up the drive;
It wasn't quite so cheery
 As when he had been alive!

I saw my cousins cleaning house;
 They had to, I was told;
As soon as everything was gone,
 The house could then be sold.

I asked about John's papers,
 Which could have filled a trunk;
They wondered why I cared so much
 For Uncle Johnny's "junk."

The grief had been enough to bear
 That Uncle John was dead,
But it left me numb all over
 As I listened when they said:

"No one wanted all that stuff;
 We burned it yesterday."
And though at first it made me sad,
 I found another way:

I now will share the hopes and dreams
 That John had shared with me,
By writing to the ones I love,
 …And all posterity!

(5/20/12)

# LITTLE GIRL

LITTLE GIRL, LITTLE GIRL,
WHY DO YOU CRY?
Because I didn't want
My grandma to die!

LITTLE GIRL, LITTLE GIRL,
WHY ALL THE TEARS?
Because I had loved her
For so many years!

LITTLE GIRL, LITTLE GIRL,
WHERE DID SHE GO?
In heaven, I think,
But I don't know.

COME TO ME, LITTLE ONE, I
ASSURE YOU SHE IS,
BECAUSE JESUS LOVES HER,
AND HER HEART WAS HIS!

LISTEN! MY LITTLE GIRL,
TO THE BELLS CHIME!
SHE'LL BE WITH OUR LORD
FOR THE REST OF TIME!

NOW TELL ME LITTLE ONE,
ARE YOU STILL SAD?
No!  Grandma's in Heaven,
And I'm so glad!

Ken and Stephanie White

# A Fond Farewell

Oh, they laid her to rest
In her best Sunday dress
And the skies were dark and clouded,

And their tears showed their pain
As they stood in the rain,
And around her casket they crowded,

And they shook with the cold,
Both the young and the old;
We'll remember our dear one forever.

Rain drummed on the tent
With a song of lament,
As we huddled in silence together!

It was hard to abide
All those feelings inside
Of loss, and sadness and joy,

But forever she'd lay
Only three feet away
From her husband and belovéd Roy.

So we bid her goodbye
As rain fell from the sky
On the last interment she'd go to,

And I turned to depart,
With a warmth in my heart;
Yes, Grandma, it's been nice to know you!

(1981)

# At Little Vermillion

I know of a place where there's nary a care,
    And peace of mind is standard fare.
I love the quiet stillness there,
    On the banks of the Little Vermillion!

Where the water's blue and the fish abound,
    And the woods are deep for miles around.
Where wind and the waves are the only sound,
    On the banks of the Little Vermillion!

At the cabin there with its lovely view,
    You can feel your spirits return anew.
It's nice what Beauty can do for you,
    When you go to the Little Vermillion!

I get a feeling beyond compare
    When the loon cries out in the evening air!
It's one of the wonders experienced there,
    When you go to the Little Vermillion!

And what can equal the thrill you get
    As you reel a trout to your landing net?
Now, that's a feeling you never forget,
    When you fish the Little Vermillion!

And how we loved to go explore
    The coves where few had been before,
To cast for bass along the shore,
    While we fished the Little Vermillion!

While the days were fun, the time would fly;
    Too soon, it seemed, we said goodbye,
But memories keep our spirits high,
    When we think of the Little Vermillion!

Here's many thanks to Ev and Lyle,
    Who kindly let us stay awhile,
And showed us how to live in style
    On the banks of the Little Vermillion!

# Nicky

Nicky was a skinny cat;
  A joy unto our dad!
His singing told us where he's at;
  His passing makes us sad.

Left lonely when his master died;
  He paced around his home.
In our lap he'd sleep, or hide
  When he'd rather be alone.

A strong one for his little size;
  He trained the dog to stay.
He was the toughest of the guys,
  But rarely did he play.

We miss his caterwauling song,
  And his pacing of the floor.
He lived a life both rich and long;
  One couldn't ask for more!

Now with his master once again,
  On a rainbow in the skies,
This little angel earned his wings,
  And the warmest of good-byes!

(11/16/10)

# Deterrent

Not all our time was on alert,
        As a combat-ready crew.
Our training took up many days,
        And twice a week we flew.

The Cold War lasted fifty years;
        While crews stood at the ready
To launch upon their final flight,
        And hope their nerves were steady!

Our country's fate was in our hands,
        Deterring other nations;
While hoping that we'd never see
        Those fearful detonations!

We carried thermonuclear bombs,
        Each destined for a city.
A war would end a billion lives,
        Without remorse or pity!

Our training showed us what to do;
        Our duties were diverse.
We couldn't falter or the world
        Would go from bad to worse!

Preparedness gave us the edge,
        To others we could boast!
As we practiced by the numbers
        For the war we feared the most!

We thought about the casualties,
　　　　The never-ending cost;
How none would be victorious:
　　　　All nations would have lost!

　　　　\*\*\*\*\*\*\*\*\*\*\*\*\*\*\*\*\*\*\*\*\*\*\*\*\*\*\*\*

Deterrence spared Humanity
　　　　Our planet's final war,
And won for us the Freedom
　　　　That we'd all been fighting for!

So, we marvel at the Cold War,
　　　　And how so few were killed!
No longer have I any doubt
　　　　How hopes can be fulfilled!

　　　　　　　　　　　　(1/8/12)

# Freedom of Flight

Like Daedelus with wings of wax,
    We've topped the sapphire sky;
As drag and thrust do counteract,
    'Tis lift that makes us fly.

To hide within the pearly wisps,
    Or soar above the earth;
To where the air is dry and crisp,
    There's freedom, joy and mirth!

Unfettered in the highest realms,
    We swing, and bank and climb;
For man indeed was made to fly,
    And flying is sublime!

Among the clouds we choose our path,
    With stars we navigate,
And plot our way with charts and math,
    To keep our courses straight!

And air refueling is a joy,
    A challenge night or day;
To stay connected to the boom,
    Without a "Breakaway!"

Alas, we land at mission's end;
    Another endless day,
Until again we shall transcend
    The earth and fly away!

(12/26/10)

# The Pass

I found within my wallet, folded, stained, with edges rough,
A paper given to me by an army history buff.


It was a pass to get a man from Ambly to Verdun
On a cold and muddy winter day in France in World War One.


Its owner was a soldier in an ammunition train
Who horsed along his wagon on a crowded, muddy lane.


This pass was signed and good from early morning until night;
I'm sure the bearer did his duty and the job was done all right.


His tunic pocket held this clue to an uneventful day;
If he meant to keep this paper, none of us can say!


It's funny how today this scrap of paper reappears
After having been forgotten for so very many years!


It's curious the artifacts we often choose to save,
Simply since their owners have been placed within the grave.


And how this fine memento, through chance and circumstance,
Preserves the memory of a cold and muddy day in Northern France!

(4/29/81)

# Brotherhood

Nothing of the things we do
    To anger one another
Would make me fail to honor you,
    Or hate you as my brother!

We often take advantage,
    When kindness is forgot;
And we're tempted to do evil,
    Instead of what we ought!

At times we drive each other
    To an angry, bitter fit;
But after far too many years,
    Perhaps it's time to quit!

When forgiveness seems impossible,
    At least we ought to try;
It might be nice to reconcile
    Before it's time to die!

So many years we've wasted,
    And our hearts refused to mend,
When we could have shared some honor
    With a loyal, trusted friend!

(7/24/11)
1 John 2:10

# Kitty Cats

I often watch our kitty cats,
      Each in his furry suit.
I wonder why the Good Lord chose
      To make them so darn cute!

I love to see their classic grin
      Beneath their button nose,
For cats inspire poetry,
      And not a little prose!

They often lie so motionless,
      As though they were a sphinx;
And cats will often smile at you
      By slowly giving winks!

You could have another animal,
      And keep it as a pet;
But raising several kitty cats,
      You never will regret!

(9/24/11)

# Renaissance Lady

As I recall my childhood,
  My closest friend indeed
Was my sister and companion,
  My dearest friend in need!

When young, she cut a noble path,
  And did what she thought right,
And gave up on the will to win
  To shun a needless fight!

She left a strict, unhappy home,
  And set her sails anew,
And took to following her bliss,
  Where winds of caring blew.

Forsaking plans of earning wealth,
  She'd doff her father's will,
And never fail to chart a trail,
  Her dreams now to fulfill!

Her children were her greatest joys,
  They learned of living well,
Her heart and wisdom both she gave
  To weave her "magic spell!"

For all the loving kindnesses
  She shared with those without,
She set a fine example
  Of a spirit so devout!

And for all her wise complexities
  She had a simple creed:
That no matter what the sacrifice,
  Of helping those in need!

She worked in corporations,
  Teaching others how to read,
And her charming personality
  Was the opposite of greed!

Her children learned of tolerance,
  With rules from up above!
She never laid a hand on them,
  Unless it was in love!

A wise and loving partner
  She is to husband Ed;
She gives considered thoughtfulness
  To everything he's said.

She learns about all aspects
  Of many fields concerned,
And got her family out of debt
  With wisdom that she learned!

She thrived at making ends to meet
  With budgeting and thrift;
Her intellect speaks volumes
  Of this never-ending gift!

How many times I'd count on her
  To mediate disputes;
Though I've heard her speak she'd rather seek
  More peaceable pursuits!

Her home is so immaculate,
  No place I'd rather go,
And from what I've heard from others,
  She is always in the know.

She's now a Lady Renaissance;
  No better will you find
In every way she doth convey
  She's gentle, wise and kind.

I can't express in meager words
  Her love so great as this
She has for all humanity,
  My loving, dearest Sis!

(5/27/09)

155

# Hopes for Heaven

If Humans go to Heaven,
    And animals do not;
Is this eternal justice
    Which all of us have sought?

When animals are "vicious,"
    They only kill for food;
But Humans will kill anything
    When simply in the mood!

For only Humankind is cruel,
    And slaughters just for sport,
While causing others dire pain,
    And wounds of every sort!

Men wildly cheer their bullfights,
    And show their love of death,
To see how poor, dumb animals
    Will take their final breath!

A man will spend an hour
    To shape a piece of log
Into an instrument of hate
    To beat his loyal dog!

It's Man alone who murders
    All life in endless wars,
And leaves the Earth in ruins,
    To settle pointless scores!

Whenever Man domesticates
    The animals as pets,
They often are abandoned, hurt,
    Or starved without regrets!

Men also have a notion,
    Instilled since time began:
To take out their frustrations,
    They can kill their fellow man.

But animals are seldom mean,
    Not in or out of season,
And will not show aggressiveness
    Without a valid reason!

If we could see the Afterlife
    Our Father has in store,
Perhaps, then, we could also see
    The "beasts" deserve it more!

Ken White (2/9/12)

# On Eagles' Wings

There's a secret that a tyrant
    Always fails to understand,
That separates the leaders,
    The average from the grand:

You cannot keep a good man down,
    Or put him in a box;
For he will make a great escape,
    As shrewdly as a fox!

Take away his freedom, friend,
    And see the wrath of God;
For men were born with choices,
    Whether true, belov'd or odd.

We laud our cherished liberty
    Against the rant and rail;
We're destined yet to overcome,
    Our Spirit shall prevail!

For love would have no meaning
    If we didn't have a choice!
Without it, there's no reason, then,
    To revel or rejoice!

There never was a homeland
    Where Freedom rang so free,
Which had so fine a heritage,
    And hope for you and me.

"Don't tread on me," once said the snake
    To nations one and all;
Just listen now, you too may hear
    Sweet Freedom's lilting call!

We're lifted up on eagles' wings,
    Above the muck and mire,
And traps and pitfalls we avoid
    To spare us from the pyre!

So tyrants knock on other doors,
    And demagogues beware!
This is no place you can debase,
    Assuming that you dare!

We're destined for a future bright
    Through endless halls of time!
We'll gather up our willing friends,
    To share a fate sublime!

(3/28/09)
Isaiah 40:31

# Living Their Faith

Elias and Eliza White
  Were grand folks very great;
They ran a secret railroad
  Underground, through their estate!

New freemen came to them at night,
  With wives and children, too,
" A' followin' the Drinkin' Gourd*,"
  Where the winds of Freedom blew!

Eliza gave them stores of food,
  So families could survive,
And new directions they could take
  To keep them all alive!

When bounty hunters made their rounds,
  Relentless, night and day,
Elias, with his golden tongue,
  Would send them on their way!

This is how they lived their faith,
  As God they would obey,
By "doing unto others," though…
  They risked their lives each day!

Of all the many wondrous ways
  To follow Heaven's laws,
Do "love your neighbor as yourself,"
  When Freedom is the cause!

(10/10/09)
Galatians 5:1

* "The "Big Dipper" (points north).

*Elias and Eliza White*

# My Brethren

I saw a man beside the road,
    Cardboard sign in hand;
He seemed to carry quite a load.
    His wrinkled face was tanned.

He had no job, so said the sign;
    Nor did he have a home.
He didn't seem to have a dime,
    But was condemned to roam!

He walked along the median,
    While back and forth he'd pace;
Burdened with the tedium,
    With sadness in his face!

I thought of giving him some bills
    I worked so hard to earn!
But would he buy some drink or pills?
    . . .What lesson would he learn?

But then, I heard the Master say
    The words that made me see:
"That what you do to the least of these,
    You do also unto Me."

(9/23/11)
Matthew 25:31-40
1 John 3:16-18

# Chapter 7 - Searching the Soul

In my quest to know God and find Salvation, I long ago came to realize that I needed to first know myself and what I really believed in, so that I might better understand how to become more Christ-like in thought, word and deed.

Although I knew Christ would accept me "Just as I Am," I continued to explore every hidden recess and corner of my mind and being. What I have found out about myself has frequently amazed and sometimes even appalled me! It remains my ongoing aim to continue to pursue the search, while doing all that I can to make all the changes required.

Through this effort, I have found a new awareness of my own shortcomings as well as the progress I am making in addressing them. I have also learned that while there are many good examples of godliness in our lives to help us to steer our course, the truest is always Christ Himself, and that in His Name, believing, we must never stop working our way toward becoming the person He wants us to be; as we constantly seek to discover and abide by "His good, pleasing and perfect will."

". . . For we are God's workmanship, created in Christ Jesus to do good works, which God prepared in advance for us to do." (Ephesians 2:10).

*Elmo*

# Respect

Forgiving must be from the heart,
    In order to be real;
And gives the only respite
    From the bitterness we feel!

For others are deserving
    Of our love and our respect,
However bad the sinner
    Or the ones whom we'd reject!

Nobody is perfect,
    And none of us would win
If Jesus hadn't died for us
    To save us from our sin!

God loves His human creatures,
    The unsaved and the blest;
It's not for us to choose the ones
    Who'll find Eternal Rest.

So, if we judge our fellow man
    Unworthy of our love,
We may be disobeying
    God's commandments from above!

(10/30/11)
1 Peter 1:22

# Building Castles

A lie is not a faithful fortress:
>When you depend on it,
It lets you down!
>We know this much about lies:
A lie is a poor thing
>To build a life on!

Like a sandcastle on the beach,
>It can only wait timorously
For the tide of Truth
>To sweep it away!

An unsaid apology is like a lie.
>It builds walls of hatred
And towers of false pride;
>But it, too, denies the Truth
Of an ocean of God's love,
>And it, too, has no right to exist!

So, what is this Truth,
>If it alone survives
On the wave-washed beach of life?

>Who knows God's Truth,
Unless it is those who know God?
>And who knows God,
But those who practice the Truth?

-    Their castles never wash away!

(2/14/86)

# What I've Learned

If all my efforts fail to show
    Respect for all my brothers,
Perhaps it means the love I feel
    Is for myself, not others!

For with some introspection,
    I often come to find:
I'm not exactly what I'd call,
    God's gift to Humankind!

And I'm not being humble,
    Or showing simple grace
By shouting at my neighbor
    To put him in his place!

Nor can I claim true friendship
    Toward others I have known,
If I think that their importance
    Is nothing like my own!

And do I view my family
    As something to *possess*,
Who live to cater to my wants,
    And suffer my duress?

And if I love my neighbor
    For what he does for me,
Then my "altruistic fervor"
    Isn't what it ought to be!

Unless I get the message:
    That it's better if I serve,
Then I'm lucky that I seldom get
    The judgment I deserve!

(1/2/11)

167

# Reconciliation II

It seems that every time I feel
    That I am ever blest,
I think of yet another sin
    That I have not confessed!

No matter how condemned I feel
    Or damned from up above,
God daily lifts me up again
    That I might know His love!

I see now when I called on Him,
    It never was in vain;
He let me struggle with my sin,
    To overcome the pain!

I know I can't excuse the way
    I treated those I knew;
But how to right the wrongs I did,
    . . . I didn't have a clue!

I thought that in believing,
    That my anguish would abate,
But the love I showed my neighbor
    Was interpreted as hate!

I knew the Lord had died for me
    To bring a life anew;
And God had sacrificed his Son
    For my neighbor too!

With wonder He had called to mind
    Remembrance of His Word,
How it was meant for doing,
    And not simply to be heard!

I looked at my relationships,
    With all my kith and kin,
And how our growth was undermined
    By unforgiven sin!

I cannot underestimate
    The damage that I'd done,
Nor the joy when God forgave me
    For my sins against His Son!

I finally opened up my heart,
    And tried to make amends,
And mailed those heartfelt letters
    On which my happiness depends!

My pastor says my efforts were
    The best that I could do
To be reconciled with loved ones,
    . . . And grow a little, too!

(11/9/11)
Luke 6:27-31

# Apologies

A matter of apologies,
  Once settled, helps us live
Without the bitter wrath that comes
  From failing to forgive!

I never would apologize;
  I thought you wouldn't mind
To suffer the offense I caused
  By being so unkind!

We tried to cause each other pain,
  (We both know this is so),
But what was it we tried to gain?
  We never seemed to know!

We never learned a lesson, though,
  As far as I could tell!
If love is blind, perhaps we showed
  How hate is blind as well!

We could have been forgiven,
  With some courage and some hope,
But behaved in such a manner
  That we simply couldn't cope!

We could have been forgiven,
  If only we had paused,
And thought of all the anguish
  And the hell that we had caused!

Nor were we ever sorry
  For the shameful deeds we did;
From our duty to be caring,
  We ingloriously hid!

Yes, we could have been forgiven,
  If only we had asked;
But instead of giving in to Love,
  We fought it to the last!

We tried to cover up our sins,
  We cheated and we lied;
We failed to show some decency,
  Because we never tried!

But Hope cannot be vanquished,
  Nor our lives be torn apart,
When apologies are offered
  With forgiveness from the heart!

(1981)

# Forgiveness: Ask and It's Yours

It would be so easy to forgive
  If only you would share the blame;
Won't you let me try to live
  Not cursing when I hear your name?

"Forgive us as we do another,"
  So we pray to God above;
But can we love a hateful "brother,"
  That's the catch I'm thinking of!

You caused me pain and much offense,
  And plunged me into deep despair;
What made the anguish so intense
  Was afterwards you didn't care!

Can I forgive you even yet?
  Is there a way to make amends?
On such things I'd even bet
  The saving of my soul depends!

We must repent and change our ways
  To avoid the awful wrath to come!
Revenge is God's and He repays,
  And we can neither hide nor run!

We never would apologize,
  And so to madness we were driven;
Time will rarely neutralize
  An ugly sin that's unforgiven!

Will we find at Heaven's gate,
  Saint Peter, waiting, full of grace;
And when we ask to know our fate,
  We'll find we both have lost the race?

(12/12/81)

# The Simple Solution

Where, O Priest, did Hell go?
    Now no one talks of Hades!
Did it go out the window
    With Gentlemen and Ladies?

Where, O where, did Hell go?
    Was punishment a fad?
Speak of sin and evil,
    And everyone gets mad!

Are situation ethics
    A substitute for laws?
Is God the Heavenly Father,
    Or merely Santa Claus?

Is anything I do okay,
    As long as I am free?
Is righteousness important,
    Or what is "right for me?"

We must make a decision
    On where we want to go;
And if we choose to follow
    The high road or the low!

So, if death for all is certain,
    And Hell is not a lie,
Then it's best we seek salvation
    Before we have to die!

# Ever Mindful

God knows the things I think about;
      He knows my every thought.
He knows when I love others, and,
      He knows when I do not!

From God I cannot hide my thoughts;
      He knows far more than I
If I should even contemplate
      The telling of a lie!

I'll try not to betray His trust,
      For God I have adored;
How in all things I know I must
      Be mindful of the Lord!

I hope to always be with Him;
      In Whom I could confide;
Where all my thoughts I'd gladly share,
      And none I'd want to hide!

And though I'm free at any time
      To seek another way;
Our God's so truly marvelous,
      With Him I'd rather stay!

Then I would know as I am known,
      And He could share with me
A wondrous, close relationship
      Throughout Eternity!

(2/19/12)

# In God We Trust

God, forgive me, I've done it again!
   I've offended another with paper and pen!
Once more I find it hard to smile,
   As I endure this time of trial!

Why do I choose to angrily speak,
   When I should be more silent and meek?
I can't believe the things I say;
   They darken even the brightest day!

I've yet to learn what anger gains;
   It merely deepens emotional pains!
And who remembers the message once told,
   When bitterness leaves the listener cold?

I try so hard to be thoughtful and wise,
   But my heart turns to stone, my message to lies!
Then I look at my work and it's easy to see
   I'm not the person I wanted to be!

But if what I wrote really had to be said,
   Why do I worry how it is read?
Is it important for me to see
   Exactly how the response will be?

If I try to do my very best,
   I'm sure that God will do the rest!
So, I will write the things I must,
   While practicing "In God We Trust!"

(12/8/83)

# Time For A Change

My youth is slipping fast away,
        I'm getting older every day.
Who stole from me the joy of life,
        The twinkling eyes, the love of play?

Now solitude's my daily fare.
        Happiness, a feeling rare;
I lose myself in futile thought,
        To keep from being too aware!

Is courage then the thing I lack
        To put my troubles at my back;
And be a friend to those in need,
        Showing love through word and deed?

(12/11/84)

# The Solution to Loneliness

If you find when you're alone
    That you are feeling blue,
Then break the chains of loneliness!
    You can! It's up to you!

First, stop and count your blessings!
    Be glad to be alive!
Let caring be your purpose;
    Give with vigor, love and drive!

Dwell upon the good things;
    Sing favorite songs aloud!
Share a happy, cheerful heart
    As though upon a cloud!

Show gladness to your neighbors!
    Share with them your joys!
End the silence you once had
    For all the girls and boys!

Reach out to all your loved ones!
    Write them! Do it first!
Make that call, and give your all!
    Yes, you can break the curse!

Allow your cup to overflow
    With love and kindness too!
It is a trusty antidote,
    When you're feeling blue!

So, when lonely and imprisoned,
    Then shatter all the walls
By sharing hope with others
    With your visits, cards and calls!

(4/9/9)

# The Presence

I once was hurt so very much,
    It was hard to find a friend;
One who had that gentle touch
    That would help my heart to mend.

I suffered quietly alone,
    And fought my constant fears,
While reaping all the hate I'd sown
    For many, many years!

The pain I had so filled my heart;
    The wounds were deep inside.
I felt they never would depart,
    To ignore them – how I tried!

Of my life I'd made a mess,
    But who would hear my plea?
I knew that if I could confess,
    The truth might set me free!

One night I got down on my knees,
    For God I had ignored;
There was no way that I could please,
    So, I waited on the Lord!

And then He came to me in prayer,
    My heart began to thaw!
His Presence left me humbled there,
    . . . In silent, breathless awe!

And so my soul began to mend;
    He healed my burdened heart!
He was for me that perfect friend
    I needed from the start!

So when you feel forsaken, do. . .
    . . . Get on your knees and pray,
To draw the Savior nigh to you,
    And evermore to stay!

(1994)
Psalm 40:1-3

# Just Desserts

This TV preacher, bold as brass,
    Begged money from the poorer class,
And entranced his listeners with his pleas,
    While asking that their alms increase!

His Father'd call him home, he'd say,
    If his sheep did not their fortunes pay.
To ransom then oneself was new,
    Which few had had the gall to do!

Now, widows gave their every mite
    To help avoid his awful plight,
And those who knew naught but TV
    Gave all they had to set him free!

And thus a fortune he did gain,
    And asked for more in dire pain!
His flock sent him their every dime,
    To end his agonizing time!

The shock of gaining all that wealth
    Then took its toll upon his health;
And knocked him flat upon his back,
    And brought about a heart attack!

And so he went on to his "home,"
    His soul no longer wide to roam!
He found himself before his lord,
    To get his due and just reward!

The story that he'd told so well
    Had made his coffers grow and swell!
The job he'd done had made him proud,
    He'd fleeced a guileless, simple crowd.

He sought his father's mighty throne,
    His pleasure in his works full blown!
His eyes rose up from bended knees,
    And there sat Mephistopheles!

(9/27/09)
1 John 4:1

# Dare I Call You Father

Dare I call You Father,
    And use Your Holy Name,
When I have sinned against Your Son,
    And He received the blame?

Was forgiveness guaranteed
    When Jesus' blood was spilt,
So there is nothing else I need
    To rid me of my guilt?

Can I correct another
    To straighten out his path;
Admonishing my brother
    To keep him from Thy wrath?

Will I show my anger,
    Once I've turned the other cheek,
When love, dismissed as weakness,
    Is the very thing we seek?

Do I have the self-control,
    When angry tempers burst,
To then forgive my enemies,
    As You forgave us first?

Shall I have the courage
    To face the ones I've hurt,
And if they demand my only coat,
    To offer them my shirt?

Shall I speak with confidence,
    When I am face-to-face
With children of impenitence,
    And tell them of Your Grace?

When I am short of answers,
    I gain and never lose,
By trusting in Your will for me,
    My path for You to choose!

And when I'm short of answers,
    Please help me to be meek,
As I pray for understanding,
    And the wisdom that I seek!

Let me trust my life to You,
    That You may lead the way;
Guiding me in everything
    I think and do and say.

(12/2/81) James 1:5

# The Lost Years

Life may seem to be unfair:
      We lost those early years;
I could not raise my daughter up;
      Divorce had left its tears!

I do regret the many times
      When I was never there;
It wasn't that I wouldn't come,
      Or that I didn't care!

I missed her first day spent at school,
      And with her Brownie friends,
Slumber parties, birthdays, too,
      And love that never ends!

Bike rides, camping, playing games,
      As well as her first date,
Helping buy her prom dress,
      And curfews, none too late!

Taking care of pets she'd say
      She'd care for all alone;
Comforting her heartbreaks
      While becoming grown!

Sharing in my feelings
      On the joy to be alive!
Helping with her homework,
      And teaching her to drive!

Adding to relationships. . .
	That little touch of mirth,
And sharing in the joy she felt
	Upon her daughter's birth!

Just to "be there" as a father,
	And to help through her divorce,
And to give my best opinions,
	(When asked for them, of course!)

Those missing years of closeness
	May be wished for now in vain;
But the love and joy that we now share
	Is well worth all the pain!

(9/30/11)

# One Sleepless Night

The Rapture came in a winking eye,
  With trumpet sounding in the sky!
I only thought of certain doom,
  When a holy presence filled my room!

And as I lay there on my bed,
  A figure came to me and said,
"Would you face your Judgment now,
  Or yet respect your Christian vow?"

"For many suffered for their Lord,
  While you complained of being bored;
And God loves those who would confess,
  But you would flaunt your selfishness!"

"He meant his teachings to be followed,
  But you in sin had always wallowed,
While acting like you'd never heard
  Suggestions that you read His Word."

"So, are you ready, friend, or not,
  For judgment of the life you've got?
Or would you choose a martyr's death
  With 'Jesus' on your final breath?"

"You'd better stay the Tribulation,
  Suffering the conflagration.
For Him you'll suffer all the more,
  With glory then for thee in store.

"The narrow path you'll have to plod,
  Lacking but the Grace of God,
Yet woe to you if you should faint,
  Or fail to be a perfect saint!"

"Think about it, say it's done
  As payment for a life of fun!
For judgment now would surely spell
  For you, eternity in hell."

I lay there, still, upon my bed.
  "Good luck, my friend," he softly said.
Before I tried a further plea,
  The room was empty, but for me!

(12/2/81)

# Abuse

To justify abusiveness
    Is cancer to our souls:
It kills the chance of finding love,
    And other worthy goals!

Abuse can be both physical,
    Or aimed at someone's mind!
And mental scars may never heal,
  -  The ugly, vicious kind!

One can't abuse a loved one
    While showing them respect;
God knows it isn't love we feel
    To those whom we reject!

There are no valid reasons
    For anyone's abuse,
To try to justify our hate
    Is only an excuse!

To claim confusion on this point
    May bring with it a cost:
That one's love and joy and righteousness
    May be forever lost!

(10/28/11)

# As We Choose

Like aging veterans who have placed their bet
    On the righteousness of their profession,
We think we have so little to regret,
    Nor have we felt moved toward confession!

What ironic justice if at Heaven's gate
    We're made to feel like heartless fools,
Reminded, "Love your neighbor," perhaps too late,
    And, "So sorry friends, but rules are rules!"

So, did they cancel my firm reservation?
    It's not like dinner at L'Aubergine!
Aren't we owed an explanation?
    Why leave our future unforeseen?

If life _is_ a puzzle, little understood,
    Let "Love thy neighbor" be your guide,
For in doing as you _know_ you should,
    You will in Heaven's laws abide!

And if through faith we're saved by Grace,
    (Unmerited favor – so immense),
Our sin the Lord shall then erase,
    Of old, today, and ever hence!

(5/19/81)
Ephesians 2:8-10
Isaiah 43:25

187

Sparky

# Chapter 8 - Stories

Every rule needs an exception, and a section of stories in a book of poetry certainly qualifies. These stories, which came into being at various points in my journey, cover a broad spectrum of topics, much as my poetry does. Allegories, campfire stories, true life, all have made their way into these tales.

The story of Rocky is just a small part of the continuing saga of his life. If you think that he may seem to hold a disproportionately large place in this book, in real life, all the beloved furry family members have equal shares, whether they are still with us, or waiting for us at the "Rainbow Bridge."

Bart, Sparky, Elmo, Lily, Dulcie, Fizzgig, et. al., all of them provide a nearly limitless supply of inspiration! In our love and nurturing of them, we also learn to love and care for each other! This, on top of the pure, unconditional love and joy they give us, more than entitles them not only to unlimited love and care from us, but also, we feel, to their share of the Heavenly joys that we all earnestly hope and pray for! After all, God is Love!

# The Wondrous Well

## A Parable by Ken White

Once there was a stone well high up in the hills that had magical, living water. For years people had been coming to the well to carefully draw out the water and place it in containers to take home. They had long known of its ability to heal those who were sick or lame! And even an old man, who had grown blind from old age, had some living water brought to him. As soon as he drank, and the water passed his lips, he not only could see again, but he now understood what he saw, which he had seldom done before!

Visitors and travelers came to the nearby villages from far off lands, having heard of the well and its wondrous properties. Naturally, the village people knew of the wonders of the well, and were all too glad that they could share some of the water with strangers. And as soon as the strangers, even the doubting ones, tasted the water, they became believers, and tried to bottle up as much water as they could carry so they could take some home to their family and friends.

The well was partly like a wishing well and partly like a fountain of youth, except that the living water made people more wise and understanding, and better able to appreciate and get along with others, while helping them to enjoy the comfort of steadfast companionship! For some reason, those who drank from the well had no enemies, and all of life thus became happier for them, and they felt that there was no reason why this state of affairs couldn't last forever!

For all it would do, this living water was regarded as precious, and naturally some greedy people who had never tried the water themselves thought they would bottle it and sell it in faraway places for a profit, but whenever someone would do this, all that ended up coming out of the bottles was ordinary water. It seemed that the magic of the living water would work only as long as the living water was free of charge. But that did not stop some unknowing people from buying bottles of ordinary water; and, needless to say, they were bitterly disappointed. So there grew up a number of people who did not believe in the living water, but thought it was all a hoax or a trick to get money from the unsuspecting.

One young girl, Jana, whose mother had unfortunately paid her last few pennies for such a bottle, was so angry at having been tricked that she decided to do something about it! She went out to the shed and took the jar of rat poison from the shelf and wrapped it in her shawl. The next day, she set out on foot toward the villages where everyone said one could get the living water. She had to walk four days, and began to understand why the peddlers charged so much; but, she thought, it was only ordinary water anyway, and the thought made her angrier!

It wasn't long before Jana was tired and she sat down on a bale of hay by a farmer's barn. She sat there for most of an hour; resting, when a man and his wife came walking from the direction Jana was headed to, carrying a bucket between them. They seemed so pleasant, and their fondness for each other seemed to radiate from both of them!

Jana asked them if the direction they came from was where the well was. "Most certainly," said the wife, "but why don't you try some of ours? It will save you a long walk!" Jana scoffed, "No thanks. I don't believe in it!" Jana thought she saw a trace of knowing sympathy and understanding in their eyes as the farmer and his wife smiled, nodded and passed on their way.

Everyone in the villages seemed to be different, thought Jana. "Why were they so polite?" Yeah, I guess I could afford to be polite, too, she thought, if I were like them and in on the joke. Her own thoughts made her angry and she hated the people now as well as the water! Jana even started to hate politeness itself; she thought it was all so hypocritical! When people tried to help Jana on her way, she was as rude to them as she could be, but they just showed sympathy and understanding, and that made Jana even madder!

The last girl Jana passed by told her that the wondrous well was just over the next hill, and in two minutes, Jana was there. It looked like an ordinary well to her, and since she was very tired, she sat down beside the well to catch her breath. Slowly, as she began unwrapping the jar from her shawl, Jana began to collect her wits. Since she was thirsty from her long trip, she thought that even ordinary water would taste good. So, Jana held the rope and unmercifully threw the bucket into the well with a snort of triumph, as she thought how in a few minutes no one would ever brag about the so-called living water again. She drew up the full bucket, but found it surprisingly easy to handle! "As soon as I drink this," she laughed, "the whole hoax will be over!"

The water looked so cool and sparkling as Jana reached into the bucket with her cupped hands. As she raised her hands to her mouth, she glanced at the jar of poison on the edge of the well and was starting to move toward it to nudge it in the well, when at that moment, as the water passed her lips; she felt a strange and wondrous sensation as though she had passed from death into life! A profound realization struck her that she had lived in a fog until now, but when she swung around to snatch the jar of poison off the wall, Jana's hand accidentally knocked the jar over the edge!

Jana stood by the well for days, telling people what she'd done, until gradually the word spread that there was no more living water besides what people had stored up in their homes. Now they offered it sparingly to closest friends and relatives.

But, to make the truth known, Jana made it her life's work going from far off village to village to tell people about the story of the wondrous living water. And those people told others, and parents told their children, and over the years each generation learned anew about the strange and wondrous water. And those stories are still being told today; for long ago it was discovered that just as the living water itself produced miracles, simply believing in the wondrous power of the living water also brings about wonderful and miraculous changes in those who believe in it! Great is the power of belief, when one believes in the right things!

# The Legend of E-ko-chee

By Ken White

Long ago, during the days of the great Indian Wars, there lived the young son of an aging chief. The boy's name was E-ko-chee, which, in the language of his tribe, meant Great Hope, because his father had such high expectations for him.

E-ko-chee, who knew that someday he was to be chief, was always given special treatment, and had become spoiled with the attention. He learned at an early age that he didn't have to work as hard and diligently as the other braves to get the same amount of recognition, while others of his age were learning the skills of hunting or the crafts they would need to know in life. E-ko-chee became a great disappointment to the tribe and to his father, but no one in the tribe said anything about it, hoping the boy would change!

E-ko-chee's father was especially troubled, because the tribes had been warring for many generations and to survive the continual attacks, his own tribe would need a very wise and resourceful chief when he himself was gone from this life. He almost regretted the name he gave his son, for he saw no great hope in the young boy. The chief tried everything he could to introduce the boy to responsibility, but E-ko-chee had no desire to accept the challenge.

Once, during a meeting of the elders in the big tent, to which E-ko-chee was invited, the old men talked about whether the Great Spirit had abandoned their tribe and there was no future for them. Now, E-ko-chee had often heard talk of the Great Spirit, but to him, that's all it was – talk! Sometimes he laughed at the old men and their beliefs.

It was later that night after the meeting that the big wind struck. E-ko-chee was amazed at its force and power. The trees bent double and the roar was sometimes deafening! E-ko-chee wandered to his favorite spot on the hill above the woods and watched the flashes of lightning light up the thundering, majestic sky! But it was getting very dark, and when E-ko-chee turned to go back to his father's tent, the ground looked unfamiliar to him. He wasn't sure which way to go, as though he'd never been there before. He wandered aimlessly for hours, fighting the howling wind, and then it began to rain. It wasn't a gentle rain, as E-ko-chee had known before, but it was rather a terrible torrent, lashed by the wind!

For the first time in his life, E-ko-chee began to feel fear. He wondered what would happen to him and called out for help, but the roar of the raging storm only grew louder. After almost being swept off his feet by the wind, E-ko-chee sat down on the ground and bowed his head to keep the wind from whipping his face, and he began to think to himself: "I am lost and at the mercy of this great wind. I am not so special now, but I am the most miserable of all those I have known." E-ko-chee was soaked and exhausted and a shivering chill swept over him. "If only…" he thought. "If only what?" he questioned, wondering what he had started to say. Then, thinking out loud, E-ko-chee tried to put his deepest desires into words. "If only there were a Great Spirit who could save me!" he called out into the wind!

Almost at once the lashing rain subsided; the wind died to a breeze, and the sky began to appear lighter. A new spirit entered E-ko-chee and he began to recognize where he was and understand the path he must take! For the first time in his life, he felt a great hope; and he began to realize that he had a destiny! Then it suddenly dawned on him that the Great Spirit was behind all this, and had been since before his name was chosen by his father!

Before long, E-ko-chee learned to be guided daily by the Great Spirit, and as he came to know about the Spirit, he taught others about Him. The young brave learned gentleness from the gentle rain; defense of the truth from the strong and persistent wind; the nobility of joyful service from the abundance of Nature, which unselfishly provides for the needs of all; and from the relentless warmth and comfort of the beaming sun, a fierce love for his people, and which he knew should fall on all the tribes of the earth!

E-ko-chee became the first of the truly great chiefs, and it is said that peace and harmony were brought to many peoples and many Indian nations who heard and understood the legend of E-ko-chee, the Great Hope, who walked with the Great Spirit!

*Rocky*

# Rocky

I'd been lying in bed for about an hour waiting for sleep to come over me and wondering about oncoming old age or whether we would ever get the bills paid up, when my thoughts began to drift to Rocky! Nothing makes me happier than thinking about Rocky, how cute he is, and how much I love holding him cuddled in my arms; face up, while I massage his furry belly. I think he actually smiles when I do it! I sometimes wonder how a person can have so much love for a self-assured, proud Himalayan cat!

Rocky was originally the prize possession of Harry, the bass player of a rock band. When Harry died at a young age, Rocky was inherited by Harry's mom, Mary, a marvelous lady and a charter member of our church. Mary was quite active in church affairs and it seems that the whole congregation got to know or know about Rocky, who was Mary's sole companion. As an "only cat," Rocky became spoiled with attention, and that is when he developed his characteristic nonchalance, and irresistible charm. As the quintessential cat, Rocky was totally loved by one and all!

Eventually, as it shall be for us all, the time came for Mary to meet her Maker, and Rocky was sent to an animal shelter. Marcia and her friend, Elaine, conducted an exhaustive search for him, spending hours on the phone each night, crying, comparing notes, and praying for success, until Rocky was finally located! Never having been exposed either to other cats or cat diseases, Rocky had succumbed to a severe respiratory infection. Nose stopped up and unable to eat, Rocky had wasted away to a shadow of his former self, when we managed to adopt him and bring him to our home.

At first, we were afraid he might not make it, and ran up thousands in animal hospital bills, although they were inconsequential if we could restore Rocky's health! For a time, he never left my room. Each morning, we checked to see if he was still alive and thanked God for granting Rocky another day of life!

He was severely dehydrated, so, with instructions from the animal hospital, Marcia learned to puncture Rocky's skin and administer fluids subcutaneously to keep him hydrated and alive until he could drink for himself. Our hearts went out to him as he struggled to survive! We knew he was beginning to recover when he started to fight off the needle!

As he showed signs of gathering strength, our hopes soared! It seemed that everyone we knew had heard about Rocky's plight. As a certain British statesman might have said, "Never in the field of human history was so much love given by so many – to a cat!" He grew more responsive day by day, and he became everybody's hero! His determination to live became legend, especially among our friends at the church, to whom he had always been so special!

To make a long story short, Rocky recovered fully, and as he got healthier, he became the most beautiful cat I had ever seen in my life! He always kept himself meticulously clean and fluffy, and his dark legs, tail and blaze across his forehead had an almost mystifying effect. He did, however, inherit some crooked teeth, and though that may have kept him from being entered in pet shows, we loved him simply for being the sweet and wonderful companion that he was, and _soo_ beautiful!!!

Rocky used to sleep on my bed beside my pillow, and I always remember him getting up and climbing upon my chest to massage my neck, as cats do. I would gently scratch his furry sides as he did it, and neither of us could have been happier. When I would wake up and Rocky was not beside me, I would call out his name, and faithfully, within two or three minutes, (if it fit with his plans), he would soon come bounding through my bedroom door! Then he would jump up on the bed, and either curl up beside my pillow for a beauty rest, or give me another of his expert massages!

When he moved over to the other house which Marcia was cleaning up after her parents died, Rocky would often hide in his new surroundings, causing everyone fits, because he had a well-earned reputation for sneaking outdoors when our backs were turned. If we called to him, however, when he did sneak outside, he would calmly wait for us to come out and bring him back in. And while he was often curious about what went on outdoors, I don't think he ever wanted to give us any real trouble.

For a number of months after being in the other house, he seemed to avoid me, and would run away when I approached him. I had to be fast to pick him up when he wandered near my feet, or he would sprint out of the room to God-knows-where! Whenever I did manage to get my hands under his front legs and lift him up, I would cradle him belly-up in my arm like a small baby, and gently massage his stomach and scratch his chin, (which he appeared to condescendingly tolerate). Rocky allowed nuzzling, but whenever I would kiss him, it was to his great exasperation and dismay. (He says it was my breath.)

Rocky is also quite the singer. I guess he picked it up from being with Harry's band. Rocky has his own special brand of caterwauling, or "singing," and he can often be heard pouring out his "dulcet" tunes throughout the house. Usually, he sings to himself on the bed in the back bedroom, though I have a sneaking suspicion he's performing for everybody's benefit. I often wonder if we recorded his songs, if they might sell on the open market; but then, I guess one would have to have a taste for such a thing!

I get a thrill when I get up from my chair and suddenly realize that Rocky had been quietly crouched there on the top of the television set, staring intently at me with his big, blue eyes! Now, when I talk to him and approach him, he seems to wait there in anticipation of me picking him up to cuddle him. When I reach for him, most other cats would jump away, but Rocky resignedly goes limp in my hands so I can get a careful grip on him to pick him up. Once situated in my arms, he calmly surveys the view from above.

To me, there is nothing nearer to Heaven than to have so close a relationship with such a marvelous creature, and enjoy his sweet company as much as I do! When I gently cradle him in my arms and stare deeply into his sparkling eyes; his bushy, chocolate-brown tail, sticking out beneath, rapidly swishes back and forth (in utter frustration). To humor me, he just lies there, looking up into my eyes, cleverly feigning love, tranquility, and perfect contentment.

Rocky is a most psychologically stable cat, if one considers that a superiority complex connotes "stability!" In accord with his egalitarian leanings, he thinks all other creatures are equally inferior; as he stalks around the house sublimely indifferent to mere humans and cats alike.

For all of his character flaws, real or imagined, I can't begin to think of what life would be like without Rocky. When the time comes for him to pass on to his eternal reward, I don't know how we will get along without him. With all he has been through, he has required an extraordinary amount of love and attention. He has brought so much joy to our household, for which we shall always be grateful!

Last night, Rocky made another of his great escapes! When my sister-in-law entered her back door, Rocky chose that as his opportunity to explore the back yard. With a flashlight, I looked for him in the dark shadows of the back yard while gently calling his name; but he was nowhere to be seen! On the second time around the house, suddenly, right in front of me, sitting in the tall grass, there was Rocky, calmly observing me with his sparkling eyes! Having been disturbed in his nocturnal sojourn, he twice voiced his protest as I brought him back into the house. We soon realized that Rocky had just been playing a game and being mischievous! It was good to know that Rocky would no sooner have run away than we would have ever gone to bed without first having found him, however long that might have taken!

Earlier, my pastor and I were discussing whether pets can look forward to going to Heaven; and interestingly, he said that there is a school of thought that suggests that they can. As the theology goes: it seems that just as mankind will be drawn into Heaven through the powerful love of God, so Nature and the animal world may too be drawn into Heaven through the special love and relationships they have with mankind!

Besides, I have an abiding belief that such marvelous examples of God's works well deserve His loving care throughout eternity and beyond!

# The Good Deed

I'd been cleaning the garage, and didn't have time to change out of my dirty (and tattered) work clothes, when I had to run out to the store. As usual, I brought along several five-dollar bills to dutifully pass out to the homeless people along the roadside on the way. I soon saw up ahead of me a person on the median, standing there with what appeared to be a cardboard sign.

I rapidly struggled to extract my wallet from my hip pocket and quickly pull out one of the five dollar bills. I had to plan my efforts carefully, because there was a lot of traffic. I did manage to avoid hitting other cars, get into the left lane beside the median, slow next to the man, and hold the five-dollar bill out the window.

He was looking in the opposite direction, so I had to honk my horn to get his attention. At first, he ignored my horn, so, desperately, I continuously blew the horn and repeatedly yelled "Sir!" over the traffic noise until he looked over his shoulder and turned around.

Only when he was facing me, did I realize that he was wearing an Armani suit, expensive wingtip shoes, and what I had thought was a cardboard sign turned out to be a quality, Italian briefcase!

Although by that time I had stopped honking the horn, he stared at me quizzically and at the five-dollar bill which I was still waving in his direction. I quickly pulled my arm in the window, but as I looked in the rear-view mirror as I pulled away, I saw him standing there staring at me with his mouth agape as though he thought I was crazy, before he turned away and continued to cross the street!

If there is a moral to this story, perhaps it is that as we seek to do our "good deeds" in life, we shouldn't take ourselves too seriously!

# Author's Note

Only when nothing was left of my career, marriage or anything else of value in my life was I finally willing to turn to God for answers! At the end of my career, I took leave to try to salvage what was left of my ruined marriage. I stayed at a religious retreat near Colorado Springs, my wife's home town. I returned to my duty station with a Jerusalem Bible I purchased at the retreat, and which I kept on my coffee table, perhaps to remind myself that at least I once had Christian origins!

I recall sitting in my living room one day, saying a silent prayer asking God what advice he might have for me in my situation. I believe that He spoke to my heart, saying that if I wanted to know His will, I might look for it in the lovely language of the Jerusalem Bible. That sounded logical to me, so for the first time, I started reading the Book of Matthew. To be honest, it all went over my head and nothing struck home until I got to a quotation from Isaiah in Chapter 13 that explained to me why my world was in the horrible state it was in – all because people refused to be converted by the Son of God! That made perfect sense to me; it certainly explained a lot of things, and it led me to become ever more dependent on God's Word for answers to life's questions. I received new revelations every time I opened the Bible's pages with a question on my mind. This, I came to understand, was how the Holy Spirit often makes the Word known to those earnestly seeking God's guidance!

Since then, I've learned that nothing takes the place of our own diligent study of the Bible to help us discover what God's will is for each of us; and that without at least a basic understanding of the tenets of our faith, we may remain as though deaf, dumb, and blind to the unlimited possibilities of close, fulfilling relationships with God and Jesus Christ! Indeed, many of the wondrous things we hear about the Christian faith turn out to be true when we accept Christ Jesus as Lord and Savior and trust in Him for our Salvation.

Even our doubts serve to help to refine and bolster our faith when we accept the Wisdom of the Lord. As we seek to follow God's wise guidance, our faith grows and deepens! When we learn to commune with God through prayerful readings of His Word, and see how life's situations soon improve as we put His teachings into action, then we know for certain that we have found the Way the Truth and the Life! Indeed, it can make all the difference in the world, and beyond!

# Kenneth W. White

Kenneth W. White was born at Ladd Field Hospital, Fairbanks, Alaska, the son of Major Maynard and Elizabeth White, on March 28, 1947. He attended schools throughout the United States and in England, graduating from McLean High School in Virginia in 1965, and from the Air Force Academy at Colorado Springs, in 1970.

Upon graduation from the Air Force Pilot Training program in 1971, Ken received his sterling wings. With fond memories of having been raised on numerous Strategic Air Command air bases, Ken chose to fly SAC B-52s at Minot Air Force Base, North Dakota, as his first duty assignment.

In 1973, Ken spent two tours of duty flying out of Guam and U-Tapao, Thailand during the Vietnam Conflict. Upon return from Southeast Asia in 1974, Ken upgraded to B-52H Aircraft Commander. In 1975, he became a SAC Command Post controller, soon to become the Senior Aircraft Controller.

After his retirement from the Air Force, and utilizing some of the initiative he learned from his father and leadership he was taught at the Air Force Academy, Ken wrote a letter to President George Bush (Sr.), suggesting that American volunteers be sent to emerging democracies and formerly communist countries to teach them the fundamentals of democratic/free-enterprise systems. Within a month, the President announced the formation of the Citizens Democracy Corps (CDC), with the same aims as those outlined in Ken's letter. Within a few short years, the CDC had succeeded in making an indelible imprint on our nation's foreign policy worldwide; having trained hundreds of people from foreign lands both in the United States and abroad in fields ranging from agriculture, to building infrastructure, to running governments.

Today, Ken still feels that goals and ideals such as those of the CDC, based on the brotherhood of man and a genuine concern for the welfare of others; rather than the habitual use of force, should become the preferred method of seeking a just and lasting world peace. To him, it remains a goal worth striving and even sacrificing for.

Ken currently is enjoying life in Northern Virginia, and looks forward to starting his next project.

CPSIA information can be obtained at www.ICGtesting.com
Printed in the USA
BVOW030712070613

322646BV00001B/1/P

9 781619 969339